D1124875

Mark,
Thank you for your
amazing jolt of positivity...
very much appreciate you!

THE LEGACY
HE LEFT ME

by Lovern J. Gordon

Editor: Jes Pan
Cover/Graphics: Laine Secrest
Photography: Dana Gibbons Photography
Cover Inspiration: Brooke Eisenhart
Typography: Diane M Serpa

Library of Congress Control Number: 2021933127

ISBN: 978-1-7346207-3-3 (paperback)

ISBN: 978-1-7346207-4-0 (hardcover)

ISBN: 978-1-7346207-2-6 (eBook)

Printed in Rephen Printing, Co., LTD in Guangzhou and the United States of America

First Printing: June 1, 2021

Paperclip Publishing LLC
1840 E Baseline Road Suite A-1
Tempe, AZ 85283

www.paperclippublishing.com

"The function of freedom is to free someone else."

— Toni Morrison

DISCLAIMER

Events mentioned are based on the author's recollection and perspective of them. Some names have been changed to protect the identity of those involved. Actual documentation from the author's restraining order and emergency room visit are included, with some information blocked for privacy of those mentioned in them.

CONTENTS

PROLOGUE

Intimate Partner Violence (IPV) or Domestic Violence (DV) is defined as physical violence, sexual violence, stalking, or infliction of psychological harm by a current or former partner or spouse.

So much of my story is derived from witnessing my father display IPV against my mother, that this story cannot be told without it. It also cannot be told without the acknowledgement that child observers of IPV inherit the trauma of what they witness. That trauma is ingrained early on, and has adverse effects into their adulthood.

I was born and raised on the island of Trinidad and Tobago which was ruled by the British until 1962, so we called our mother Mummy, a culturally relevant term of endearment. My father, on the other hand, didn't believe in nicknames and insisted that we all call him by his first name, Lloydie (LOY-dee).

My siblings and I were conditioned from an early age to view our mother as "less than," based on how our father treated her. It wasn't until years later that I realized she was much stronger than I had ever given her credit for, based on the fortitude and resiliency it took to make it through all he had done to her.

After high school, Lloydie went on to be trade school educated and possessed the ability to help his children with school work. He was the breadwinner who supported our family financially. He was also Mummy's brutal abuser for the 32 years they were married. In stark contrast to her husband, Mummy barely had an elementary school education. She worked as a housekeeper when my father mandated that she was allowed to, rarely read, and did not keep up with current events. In her eyes, she would never be as intelligent as he was. Her place was in the home, tending to the children and making sure Lloydie was pleased at every juncture.

Mummy thought she was giving us a fighting chance at life by enduring his emotional abuse, verbal tirades, and physical beatings. She hoped his articulate way of speaking, intelligence, and love of reading would rub off on her children and make us all well-rounded adults. She did not understand that my siblings and I felt hurt and helpless every time we saw our father "put her in her place." Anything she thought he did right really didn't matter to us. His negative traits seeped into us like a cancer, searing the violence into our brains for the rest of our lives. We were all left with a skewed idea of love, which would follow us into relationships as adults. This path was set up for us by Lloydie long before we had any choice in the matter.

CHAPTER 1:
Cute and Romantic, Right?

Lloydie and Mummy met in 1973 when they were both nineteen years old on their home island of Trinidad, where they would remain to raise our family. She was immediately infatuated with his intellect, charisma, and outward confidence. He wore this mask well, so the evil that lay beneath would not come to light until he had her wrapped around his fingers. A few months after they met and began living together, Lloydie set the real tone for their long marriage with jealous tirades and verbal put-downs. The social butterfly my mother was prior to meeting him eventually dwindled to meekness in his presence.

My parents were married at City Hall about three years after they met. He surprised her one day by telling her to get dressed because he wanted to take her downtown. Excited, she got dressed for their date in a fashionably casual outfit. When the taxi let them out, she saw they had arrived at City Hall where he already had a witness and Justice of the Peace waiting. After she saw all of this, he asked her to marry him. Though still in shock, she was tickled pink and agreed to the impromptu wedding. Sounds cute and romantic, right? Hold that thought, because there will be more on that later.

Though we lived in a poor part of town, our family was considered lower middle class. Lloydie was the first in his family to attend and graduate vocational school right after high school, and went on to make a decent living working for the Department of Labor. Even though his job afforded him a comfortable salary, he was quite meager as a provider, only dishing out the basics: books required for school, one school uniform and pair of shoes per child, and food in our bellies. We did not have alternate clothes to wear while relaxing at home or for the occasional outing, and we were not allowed to participate in any extracurricular activities that cost money. We were not allotted money to buy lunch or snacks at school, since we were part of the government's lunch program. Any occasional extras came from extended family members or hand-me-downs that Mummy acquired from friends.

Even though my parents rarely displayed their affection outwardly toward each other, I understood from early on that there was an undeniable love between them as a couple. If he was in a good mood, Lloydie would randomly spin and dance with Mummy around the living room as the record player spilled out tunes like The Drifters' *Under The Boardwalk* or one of his favorite songs by Calypsonian artist Sugar Aloes. They also sometimes got all dressed up to go out with friends, Mummy looking stunning and Lloydie effortlessly dapper. I lived for times like this where they looked happy, full of life, and downright regal. Their excitement on nights like this rubbed off on everyone in our house, hinting at peace for the whole family. My siblings and I always hoped this meant the good times were here to stay. Unfortunately, the other shoe always had a tendency to drop, just when my childish hope convinced me that the happiness would last.

***

I was born in 1977 and raised in a town called Laventille, located just outside Trinidad's capital, Port of Spain. Trinidad is the southernmost island in the Caribbean and sits a stone's throw away from the country of Venezuela. It is known for its diverse culture, being a regional leader in financial services and energy, being the largest exporter of oil from the Caribbean to the United States, and for its yearly dynamic Carnival celebrations.

My four siblings and I had all the common experiences of growing up on an island. We took impromptu showers in the rain, walked a mile to our school everyday in groups, enjoyed delicacies like Pelau and Curry Roti, ate fresh tropical fruits from trees in the neighborhood, played sports like soccer and cricket, and listened to Soca music. You name it, and if it was allowed, we did it.

Oddly enough, one of the things our childhood lacked were visits to the beach. This was a huge part of island life we missed out on, simply because Lloydie did not see value in taking us. He was never big on family outings and never let the family ride in any of his cars, consistently concerned that we would get the vehicles dirty. To this day, I cannot swim.

I came to understand in early childhood that Lloydie was powerful, smart, and effortlessly commanded respect. My siblings and I watched our mother shower him with loads of it, so we did the same. We also feared his presence if he was in a bad mood, just as our mother did. Even if he was in a good mood, we still proceeded with caution. He was athletic with a mean backhand slap and strong legs used for soccer in public and disciplinary kicking behind closed doors.

I was the middle child of the five children. In 1985 my one and only sister, Annalise, was thirteen, my oldest brother Bronson (Bron for short) was eleven, I was eight, my younger brother Sean was five, our youngest brother Javan was an infant. It was petrifying to watch the way Annalise and Bron were beaten or scolded if they ever stepped out of line, made a mistake, or didn't measure up to Lloydie's standard of being "good kids." His abuse of my two oldest siblings was not as severe as the punishments he dealt our mother, but I still witnessed them being beaten with things like 2x4 pieces of dimensional lumber and thick electrical cords. During his assaults on them, Lloydie sometimes kicked them after they were already immobile on the ground, crouched in the fetal position with their hands protecting their heads. I would peek in from another room as Lloydie

Lloydie pictured in lighter top (top, right), captain of his neighborhood soccer team

attacked them, wishing and praying with all my might that I could make him stop. Witnessing this was enough for me to know that I wanted none of what our father was dishing out.

I realized there were some things we could do that made him pleased with us. My siblings' perceived "mess-ups" helped me register that I needed to do the opposite of whatever he saw as unfit in them. In doing so, I would receive his approval for doing well in school, helping Sean with his homework, taking pride in my chores, being polite to our neighbors, and memorizing my nightly prayers, including the popular 23rd Psalms Chapter that I learned from attending church weekly. In part, it read: *The Lord is my shepherd; I shall not want. He maketh me to lie down in green pastures: he leadeth me beside the still waters. He restoreth my soul: he leadeth me in the paths of righteousness for his name's sake.*

I never understood why me being able to recite this particular piece of the Bible made any difference to him, since he very rarely attended the church Mummy took us to each week. Still, it was important to him that I take Sunday School seriously. I learned to pray there and practiced it quietly when I was by myself, often asking God to make our nightmare end.

Though I feared him deeply, I also yearned for his fatherly affection, so I did all that was required and then some while trying to steer clear of his monstrously violent side. Even though he sometimes praised me for acting my best, there still was a huge lack of the tenderness I observed being displayed on TV sitcoms. As rough as the characters had it on shows like *Good Times*, episodes still ended with hugs and verbal declarations of love. I craved that.

At the end of the day, I rationalized that at least he didn't beat me the way he beat Mummy and my older siblings. That had to be enough.

***

Prior to meeting Lloydie, Ms. Jenifer Samuel was a department store model who even landed a couple of fashion segments in the local newspaper. Even after she stopped modeling and married Lloydie, Mummy's beautiful dark brown complexion continued to blend perfectly with everything she wore as if she were ready to strut down a runway at any time.

Mummy during a night out with Lloydie

IDEAL FOR TWILIGHT HOUR

THIS creation is the ideal outfit for twilight. A soft flowing gown of patterned Quiana, is worn by Jennifer Augustine. It features a demure round neckline, no sleeves and that popular clipped hemline. It's the type of outfit which is just right for evening relaxation, whether it's at a formal or informal party.

The evening after our youngest brother Javan was christened, our parents hosted an intimate gathering of some close family and friends to commemorate the occasion. Mummy wore a black, knee length, fitted trumpeted skirt with blue polka dots at the bottom. She paired the skirt with a black tank top, red necklace, red open-toe heels, rouged cheeks, and burgundy lipstick. It all complimented her hourglass figure and she looked stunning. Whenever I saw her in that light, I wondered to myself why Lloydie didn't cherish her more or treat her better. Why didn't he show her physical affection more frequently? Why did she stand for the abuse? In my eyes, she could have anyone she wanted.

Based on the way Lloydie treated her, my siblings and I surmised that she could be taken less seriously whenever she requested we do something. We

*Mummy holding Javan on the day of
Christening in the family's living room*

saw her as subservient, "less than" in comparison to our father. He would belittle her in front of us, calling her things like illiterate and stupid, and using the most vile curse words. We witnessed this so often that Sean and I could fluidly recite the horrible words while reen-acting his attacks on her in a lighthearted, funny manner as part of our child's play.

In addition to his verbal, emotional, and physical abuse, Mummy was overworked from Lloydie's constant demands. She rarely slept through the night, and she suffered from severe asthma attacks that landed her in the emergency room many times. Through it all, she beamed with pride at the fact that hey children had someone smart like him around. It was as if she had accepted that she would never be on his level. The whole family was painfully aware of this dynamic in their marriage. I deeply and quietly resented her for it.

That resentment was fueled by my love of shows on television like L.A. Law, where I first saw actor Blair Underwood's lawyer character, Jonathan Rollins. Underwood's assertiveness in the role resonated with me, because

I recognized some of the strengths he possessed were strengths I also admired about my father. Strengths I hoped to exude one day. Then there was actress Phylicia Rashad's Clair Huxtable character from *The Cosby Show*, who was also a lawyer, and who also resonated with me because I wanted to be as strong and assertive as she was. I would think to myself, *If only Mummy would be more like Clair Huxtable she could stand up for herself.* The confidence these characters exuded, their self-assurance and poise, spoke to me every time I saw them on our TV screen. I wanted to grow up to be a lawyer like them, so I could defend Mummy against Lloydie in court one day just as they did for their clients.

One of the pastimes for the kids in our neighborhood was a game called Judge and Jury, where I always wanted to be the prosecutor. My role in the game sought to prosecute men like my father, criminals who beat their children and treated their wives like banished dogs. Pretending to sentence Lloydie and throw away the key always felt liberating. I loved pretending to see him get what he deserved, even if it was only a game. I was much too small to take him on physically when he targeted my mother or older siblings, but in the perfect world of Judge and Jury, I could legally unleash on him the pain he physically inflicted on them. I delivered courtroom sentences so brutal, he wouldn't be able to hurt anyone ever again.

One of my other escapes was music. When Prince's video for *"When Doves Cry"* was released, I believed in my heart of hearts that I too could grow up to take on my abusive father. The part of the music video where Prince pulls his father off of his mother during a violent attack stuck with me. I believed I could be that defender for Mummy one day, in a courtroom setting. That, however, was all in my head. When the games and music videos were over, I was always left with my bitter reality.

My reality meant that I had to drop the facade of the capable, assertive lawyer and go back to being a fearful and polite child when Lloydie walked in the door and decided to randomly start verbally assaulting my mother. Reality was the twisted feeling in the pit of my stomach when Lloydie was getting ready to physically hurt her. Reality was Lloydie yelling and cussing at the top of his lungs from another room while arming himself with household weapons or balling up his fists in front of her, viciously accusing her once again of cheating, accusations that were always unfounded. Every time he attacked her I would wonder how bad the beating would be this time, or if she would be able to escape quickly enough to avoid it. My reality meant that the only thing I could do was hold my breath and pray for it to end.

When she managed to escape Mummy would run out of the house, sometimes barefoot, to a friend's house where she would stay until the coast was clear. In the years before Javan was born, Sean and I would some-times quietly beg her to take us with her while Lloydie ranted and raved in another room. If it was a weekend and we didn't have school the next day, she would sometimes hurriedly oblige us. The three of us ran quietly in tandem, usually ending up at one of her friends' houses where we would be safe for a night or two. Sometimes Lloydie found us and would come in on his best behavior, knowing Mummy's friends were strong and assertive. He would beg her to come back home, vowing in an unusually quiet tone that this time things would be different. He told her that her staying away any additional amount of time was not needed, because he would do her no more harm to her going forward. These manipulation tactics worked well on her each time. While packing up to take us back to the house of pain, I would hear her telling our hosts that she couldn't take care of us on her own financially, and that things were "all good" now, so it was okay for us to return home. I wouldn't have minded never going back and being homeless if it meant that we didn't have to return to Lloydie.

If there was no avoiding an attack from him, he would commence punching and kicking her all over her body and head or stomping her with his feet while she was on the ground. He might also drag her through the house by her hair or limbs until she was cornered in a room, or out onto our front yard where he would continue the beating on the concrete ground. He sometimes used a machete while beating her outside, whipping her with the flat part of the huge curved sword. Mummy's cries were gut wrenching as she begged and pleaded with him to stop, but they always fell on deaf ears.

If the police were notified by a neighbor who had a landline telephone (we did not at the time), one or two male officers would show up and ask Lloydie what happened. He always had an articulate response, usually citing a domestic misunderstanding, and the cops would dismiss the conflict as "a husband and wife thing." Never any help there.

Neighbors would sometimes come out of their houses to watch with horrified looks as he beat her outside our house. Some of them were men he hung out with on our street after work. These men were his size or bigger. To me, they could and should have physically stopped him from attacking her. Frustration didn't even begin to cover the way I felt when they didn't. What I did not yet understand was that some of those men also beat their girlfriends or wives behind closed doors. They never interfered with Lloydie because that would be telling another man how to run his house. Even though I was being raised with the completely accepted idea that you somehow garner respect from the person you love by beating and berating them, it was utterly crazy to me that the people around us had accepted this abusive behavior as the norm.

There was one man who moved into the neighborhood with his family and provided me with a little bit of hope. He and Lloydie became friends and had many similarities, except this man never laid a hand on his wife. When I found out he was a devout Christian and a policeman, I thought, *This is great! He will see or hear Mummy getting beaten and he'll come and arrest Lloydie!* The man seemed to be serious about upholding the law otherwise, so I was certain our hell would come to an end with this policeman living nearby. The problem came when I found out that the man was usually at work when the beatings occurred. Almost every time Lloydie came after Mummy, the officer was at work and my hopes that he would save her and arrest him were always dashed.

By the time they were in their teens, my oldest siblings had gotten to their breaking point with the child abuse. Bron was so mentally affected by the beatings he received and witnessed that he began lashing out in anger at his peers and adults in authoritative positions. He was expelled from two different high schools and joined a neighborhood gang. One night, prior to being expelled from the second school, I overheard Mummy telling Lloydie that Bron's teacher had suggested he see a "head doctor" (psychiatrist).

"He ain't fucking crazy," Lloydie responded angrily. "I ain't paying for none of that shit. He just needs more licks on his ass to straighten him up!" By licks, he meant beatings.

Around the time Bron joined the gang, he also started physically retaliating against our father. It became clear that he and my father could not coexist in the same space. Bron moved into one of the rooms of the house next door, that our father also owned and rented out to tenants.

Mummy couldn't afford a psychiatrist for Bron on her own, so she turned to the next best thing to help her son: prayers. Not just getting on your knees to pray or taking us to church every Sunday and asking the Pastor to pray. Mummy made the trek to Mount Saint Benedict, a church run by monks located in the hills of a town called Tunapuna, located about 30 minutes by car from where we lived. There, she received what I perceived to be "super prayers" from the monks. My mother had never learned to drive, so the trip to the hills involved lots of walking and at least two different taxis. She said the "super prayers" were to save my brother, but I always wondered if she ever asked for an extra one that would make Lloydie a better father and husband.

After a few years of Bron being in the gang, it seemed as though the super prayers had begun to work. He got out of the gang alive, when many of his friends had been arrested or killed. He saved up his money and built a corner store on our street which he still owns today, and never returned to gang life. As Mummy would say, "Thank you Fadda God!" Those super prayer trips were really worth it!

My one and only sister, Annalise, received her last beating in 1987 when she was sixteen. She fled the attack, hightailing it barefoot out of the house without looking back, and never returned to live at home again. I saw Annalise as very attractive, with beautiful straightened hair like Mummy's. Unlike our mother she projected assertiveness, especially when Lloydie wasn't around. I had always known my sister wanted to be done with the horrible hand she was dealt. I saw the desire in her eyes. Annalise was silent a lot, but seemed to come alive after painting her long, natural nails while singing a Whitney Houston song or being able to leave the house to run an errand for one of our parents. We didn't have much in common because of our five-year age gap, and I knew that Annalise and Bron saw that Lloydie beat me and our younger siblings much less than he beat them. I was secretly happy when she ran away and didn't come back. Not because I wanted her to, but because I knew he couldn't hurt her anymore.

Once Annalise left, the youngest three of us were left: Sean, Javan, and myself. I turned ten in 1988 and my father's continued admiration for my good deeds at home and school manifested into him allowing me to spend the summer months at my

Annalise

Godmother's and cousin's homes. They both lived in more well-to-do areas of the island. I was never excited to return home after visiting them, because I knew the tensions that awaited me there. I would once again have to walk on eggshells and be extra, extra good to avoid triggering Lloydie. Whenever I returned home Sean, who was two years younger than me, would get me caught up on the funny neighborhood news I had missed. He would also remind me with his unobtrusive body language and downcast eyes that things were still exactly the same in our house, citing attacks on Mummy that I had also missed.

Being awarded with the time away in nicer neighborhoods was not only exciting, but an opportunity to show extended family that I was not just the little girl whose father beat her mother in the streets of the ghetto where we lived. I could also speak articulately and be polite and responsible in an effort to please my more affluent family members. I would watch the dynamics of their families and think to myself, *This looks a little bit more like the families on TV. They say "I love you" here. They hug here. I really wish they would keep me here.*

***

Adverse Childhood Experiences, or ACEs, are potentially traumatic events that occur during childhood (0-17 years). Things like:
- experiencing violence, abuse, or neglect.
- witnessing violence in the home or community.
- having a family member attempt or die by suicide.

While the last bullet point was not an ACE I experienced, the top two were incredibly normalized in our community. Without Mummy or I knowing that ACEs were even a thing, there was no solid information for why I was a chronic bedwetter until my early 30's. Yes, you read that right. For so many years, I was ashamed of it. As a child, I would wet the bed after a recurring nightmare where I fell from a high cliff at night into an abyss of darkness. I would then awake suddenly, feeling wet, and realize I had saturated my part of the bed with piss. I shared a bed with Sean, and would always try to hide the mess or clean it up before anyone realized what had happened. As a light sleeper, Mummy usually realized I was up and assisted in the clean up before Lloydie awoke to any of our puttering about. I was frustrated as to why this was happening, because I wasn't drinking any fluids close to bedtime and couldn't think of any other reason why I wet the bed so frequently.

Without knowing about ACEs, I also could not understand why I suffered from severe asthma attacks the same way Mummy did. The attacks got me frequent visits to the local ER, because my prescribed inhaler was never strong enough to combat them. I felt guilty when the attacks came on because it meant Mummy would have to take me to the hospital amidst everything else she was dealing with, but despite my tight chest and limited ability to breathe, I loved the adventure away from the house. Lloydie gave her transportation money to get us there because he refused to take us in his car. When we arrived at the hospital they always followed the same process: nebulizer treatment until I was able to begin to breathe on my own, then send me back home with clear lungs.

According to the CDC, toxic stress from ACEs can change brain development and affect how the body responds to stress. Basically, your body keeps a count of all the trauma it receives directly or indirectly. This toxic stress can be linked to chronic health problems and mental illness. This was the reason for my violent nightmares, bedwetting, and severe asthma attacks, but this explanation would not become apparent until many years later.

***

Our maternal grandparents were well aware of all the abuse their daughter faced over the years. Antia and Pappy, as we nicknamed them, had migrated to the United States in the 1970's. Many of Mummy's siblings still lived in Trinidad and were in close contact with her, so they would report back to their parents about the abuse to which Lloydie subjected Mummy early in their relationship. Before my parents were married, our grandparents wrote Mummy a letter stating that they would file immigration paperwork for her to escape and leave him. Lloydie intercepted that letter when it arrived, never showed it to her, and subsequently set up their whole surprise wedding in the weeks that followed. Once they returned home from their nuptials in February of 1974, he read the letter aloud to her and then burned it in front of her, stating, "You belong to me now. If they ever wanna get to you, they'll have to go through me." This was the beginning of their incredibly uneven power dynamic and the high level of control he already had over her.

Over the years at Christmastime, Antia and Pappy would supply each of their kids' families with toiletries and basic clothing in bulk. Our father was quite greedy financially and did not buy basic things like this for us, so the gifts from our grandparents always seemed like gold to us. Everything was brand new and American-looking.

I had never met my grandparents in person, and had only seen a few pictures of them over the years. Even though they lived thousands of miles away, I never wanted them to see me in a pitiable light based on what they knew of our plight with Lloydie. I wrote long letters to them about how well I was doing in school, the praises I received for my grades, and the fun things I saw on American TV shows that I dreamt about doing if I ever got a chance to visit. Writing to them served as another form of escapism outside my lived reality. I always hoped that when they read my thank you letters each year, it would paint a picture for them of my escape from Trinidad.

1993, the year I was set to turn sixteen, is when the seemingly impossible happened. Lloydie received a letter from my grandparents saying they thought I had the potential to flourish academically in the States because of my book smarts, and they wanted to give me the opportunity to finish high school there. In the letter, they asked if he would allow me to travel with my aunt and cousin, who were also going to migrate later in the year, and stay with them while I attended high school.

Lloydie read the letter aloud in the presence of Mummy and I. Once he finished, he asked me with a slight smirk on his face, "What do you think?"

I was speechless and wasn't really sure if it was a trick question meant to gage my level of loyalty to our family or if the wrong answer could warrant a backhand slap. To be on the safe side, I shrugged my shoulders in response as if to say, *I'll abide by whatever you think is best.* To my absolute surprise, Lloydie said that he thought it was a good idea, and he would start the VISA process for me to travel.

Did he really just say what I think he said? I thought. *He's really gonna let me go? Out of his sight, thousands of miles away? Away from all this? Away from him?*

Mummy was ecstatic about my opportunity to go live in the States. It took a few minutes for me to register that the words had actually come out of Lloydie's mouth, but I eventually accepted that the process was indeed happening. The next few weeks went by in a blur with embassy visits, appointments for passport photos, notarizing all my documents, and being stuck with needles for necessary vaccines. Lloydie moved swiftly, never delaying any task he had to do on his end to make my grandparents' request a reality. Every step of the way, I was shocked. Here was my father, really showing how much he believed in my potential.

Before I knew it I was at the Piarco Airport, about to walk away from my family and onto a plane for the very first time, along with my aunt and cousin. Excitement bundled with nerves, and I was also sad to leave my family. For the first time ever, I shared a hug with each of my family members. Also for the first time, Lloydie stated that he believed I was capable of doing well and that he had faith in me. With one final stern warning from my father to do my best while in the States, I was off. My heart ached that I was leaving Mummy, Sean, and Javan with him, but I also harbored a secret selfishness that I would never have to return to living in his terrible home. Although I was stepping into the unknown, this thought brought me joy.

According to the Center for Disease Control (CDC), about 61% of adults surveyed across 25 states reported that they had experienced at least one type of Adverse Childhood Experiences (ACEs), which includes being a child witness to domestic violence or Intimate Partner Violence (IPV).

For example:
- *experiencing violence, abuse, or neglect*
- *witnessing violence in the home or community*
- *having a family member attempt or die by suicide*

Children growing up with toxic stress may have difficulty forming healthy and stable relationships. They may also have unstable work histories as adults and struggle with finances, jobs, and depression throughout life. These effects can also be passed on to their own children. Some children may face further exposure to toxic stress from historical and ongoing traumas due to systemic racism or the impacts of poverty resulting from limited educational and economic opportunities.

CHAPTER 2:
A New Life

I arrived in the States in the summer of 1993 with my Aunt Claire, Mummy's younger sister, and her daughter. From the time we landed at the airport in Miami for our connecting flight to Boston, I fell in love with the fast pace of things and watching people hurry to and fro to get to where they needed to be. So much diverse food, so many different accents… I loved it all!

I was finally going to meet my grandparents, Antia and Pappy, after only seeing them in pictures over the years. I would also get to see my Aunt Bianca again, the youngest of Mummy's siblings, who I knew briefly in Trinidad before she migrated in the 80's. Pappy picked us up in Boston with his grand Lincoln Town Car, greeting each of us with a warm bear hug. He looked exactly like his pictures, except for the new addition of an extra round belly. Even though rain was pouring nonstop, Pappy still tried to give the three of us a rundown of each landmark we passed on the way back to the house. His happiness that we had arrived was palpable. His positive attitude made me equally giddy with excitement as I listened to him and Aunt Claire catch up amidst the tour of the city he loved.

We pulled up to the house, and it looked like a three-story castle to me. We had to run from the car to the front door because it was still pouring rain. Antia and Aunt Bianca welcomed us at the door. There were more hugs that immediately made me feel at home. After the hubbub of getting inside and settling in, Pappy and Antia gave us a tour of the house and showed us our rooms. My cousin and I shared a good sized bedroom where I had my own bed. This was new for me as I had always shared a bed with my younger brother, Sean. Later that evening, we all sat around the large table in the kitchen like a TV family to eat dinner. We talked, laughed, and enjoyed each other's company. I pinched myself several times that first night to make sure it wasn't all just a dream.

Over the next few weeks we settled into the house, collected information about signing up for school, and visited the neighborhood health center for check ups. I was eager to attend school and show my extended family that

I could earn my keep with good grades. This was one of the only ways I knew to express gratitude and love, and hopefully receive love and admiration in return.

With my Aunt Bianca living on the second floor and the third floor of the house rented out, I lived on the first floor of the three-family home with my grandparents, Aunt Claire, and her daughter. The house was located in a town called Dorchester, fifteen minutes outside the city of Boston. The neighborhood was lovely and all the neighbors I'd met so far were very friendly. Antia kept a small garden at each side of the porch entrance, where she tended to tomato plants and rose bushes weekly during the warmer months. After a while, I started joining her in the garden to help, and could immediately see why she loved doing it. Along with being able to chat with people as they passed by, I found getting my hands in the dirt extremely therapeutic. I also loved spending time with Antia, listening intently as she taught me about the care and keeping of each plant.

That fall, I entered the tenth grade and flourished academically and socially. I even picked up an American accent! I joined school clubs, sat on the debate team, and was well liked by my teachers and peers. I never suffered another asthma attack after migrating to the States, which seemed like an overnight miracle. This enabled me to run track and field and play JV Basketball after school without feeling like I was fighting for my life, gasping for air and unable to breathe. I had no explanation for my asthma's sudden absence, but I was not complaining.

Even though life in the States was so much better, my childhood nightmares had progressed into another horrific recurring scene. The dream started with me at eight years old, sitting next to Lloydie in the living room on an accent chair at our house in Trinidad. I was forced to watch him slice Mummy slowly with a switchblade as she lay flat on her back, immobile on the couch. She writhed in pain, moaning loudly with every cut she endured. My dream-self would scream, yell, and plead at the top of my lungs for him to stop, but no sound ever came out of my mouth. When I awoke suddenly in the middle of the night, I would again be in a pool of piss. At least now I was in a bed of my own that I could quietly clean up with no fear of being beaten.

How could I still be peeing in my sleep? I thought. *I am a fully functioning teenager, still wetting the bed!* I never told any of my extended family members about the nightmares or the dreams because I didn't want to be a concern to anyone, so I continued to clean my sheets in secret and bottle up my emotions.

Over the next three years, I barely called back home since I knew Lloydie would most likely answer the landline they had installed shortly after I migrated. Instead, I waited for my mother to call from another house where she could talk freely. From time to time, I overheard my grandparents and two aunts discussing news they had received about Mummy fleeing more attacks, or how they were again trying to file immigration papers to get her away from him for good. I never asked any of them about the progress of getting Mummy to Boston, because I believed Lloydie would never let her go.

***

I turned 18 in 1995 and my grandparents and aunts threw me a surprise birthday party attended by family and friends. It was the only party I had ever had, and it's a memory I hold it near and dear to my heart. I graduated high school in May of 1996 after attending a memorable prom that my family also made sure was a very special occasion.

Just prior to graduation, I was told that I would be going back to Trinidad later in the year. My grandparents had filed immigration paperwork that would grant Mummy, Sean, Javan, and I permanent residency status in the States. This meant I had to return to the island so I could attend pertinent appointments at the embassy with my parents. I was heartbroken about having to return. I had become accustomed to my new life, made friends, and done well in school. I dreaded going back to the environment I despised, even if it was temporarily, but had no choice in the matter if I ever wanted to become a permanent resident of the United States.

When I arrived in Trinidad later that summer, I was not the same girl that had left the island three years prior. I was much more assertive, and felt I was just as smart as Lloydie. Although I was still a little fearful of him, I knew I could level with him and maybe even win an argument. One afternoon about a week after I returned, I overheard him verbally abusing Mummy. He was in the kitchen, yelling at her while she and I were in the living room. Anger swelled in my veins as I listened to his voice get louder and louder. Is he really still doing this? I thought angrily.

Lloydie entered the living room where Mummy and I sat together watching TV. He began to advance slowly, his steps getting smaller as he drew closer to her. I watched her presence get tinier and tinier in fear. His body looked tense, fists balled up at his sides. I instinctively got up and stood between them, to his surprise as well as my own.

Facing Lloydie with my back to Mummy, I was terrified. At this moment I thought he would hit me or push me out of the way. Instead, he actually backed up a few steps! It was enough to let me know he wasn't going to strike me for blocking him from assaulting his wife. I felt strong and resolute in defending her, but still didn't know if Lloydie would decide to lash out at me for being defiant. I stepped away cautiously and poked my head out the front door to yell out for my older brother Bron, who still lived next door, to come over and back me up.

Bron was now taller and stronger than Lloydie. He did not stand for our father putting his hands on Mummy if he was around. He immediately came running over when I called out to him. When he arrived, he and I both confronted Lloydie. "You can say what you wanna say," we told him, "but don't you dare put your hands on her!"

Looking at our father's face, it was obvious he was furious that his kids were standing up to him. The anger in his eyes screamed as we stood before him, blocking him from her. After my brother and I reiterated our firm message a couple of times, Lloydie began to threaten that he would burn the house down because of our blatant disrespect toward him. He grabbed a box of matches and started trying to light them in hopes of setting the window curtains ablaze. As much as he tried though, none of the matchsticks he struck at the side of the box gave so much as a spark. After about four attempts, he gave up in frustration, threw the box to the floor of the living room, and stormed out of the house. Bron and I had protected our mother! I was empowered at this shift in the house, and I could tell Mummy was relieved. It was an epic turning point I believe, him realizing that she had an army ready to fight on her behalf, that I could assimilate at any time. It was no longer business as usual.

Lloydie did not return until much later that night, and when he did, he walked in drunk. Over the years Lloydie had sometimes decided to get drunk on his bimonthly pay days, and we were always grateful that he wasn't a violent drunk. He would mostly be unusually generous with money, leave money lying around, and babble on with slurred speech about whatever he had on his mind. Then, he would pass out until morning. I liked Drunk Lloydie much more than his sober counterpart.

Returning home that night, he drifted a little from left to right in the entryway, trying his best to keep his balance. He started rambling about Mummy, Bron, and me being disrespectful to him earlier that day, and how he expected more from me. I rolled my eyes, but simultaneously felt a sort of sickened sorriness for him. I mean, this man was angry because he couldn't beat on his wife because his kids would protect her from him. Hearing him go on and on, implying that if my brother and I had just stepped back to let him have his way, all would have been right with the world, was not only pitiful, it was downright sickening.

After a while he said he was tired and wanted to go to bed, so Mummy helped him get to the bedroom where he slept till morning. Whenever he woke up from one of his drunken stupors, Lloydie usually didn't remember much from the night before. Because of this, we knew there would not be a repeat of his "trying to burn down the house" threat. Yesterday was yesterday, and we could leave it there.

Early that afternoon, Lloydie stood in front of the house waiting for a friend of his to arrive. I saw he was in a good mood, so I decided to seize the opportunity to strike up a conversation with him. I needed answers. It was time for me to understand where the monster we had endured all those years had come from, and why it even existed.

As I headed out the front door to talk to him, I clutched my belly with anxiety and anticipation. I was nervous and not quite sure how I was going to start. Would he curse at me in response? Strike me? Would one of my brothers, all located in and around the house at the time, have to step in to get him off me? I continued to approach him despite the very real possibility of any of these scenarios playing out. As I approached him outside, he turned to me with a smile on his face. Drinking the night before had worked magic on his next day's demeanor.

Standing next to him, I started out by asking, "How are you enjoying the weather?" I could not believe that was the opening line I came up with. Blame it on living in Boston for three years, where nice weather depended on the season and the person you were asking. It was a common pleasant question to pose to anyone, but I sure wasn't in the States anymore.

"It's alright," Lloydie replied with the same little smile.

What I am about to say is not easy for me, is what I wanted to tell him. This was the first time that I had attempted to initiate any kind of conversation with him, but I wanted to address the beatings. Even though I was nervous, I believed with everything inside of me that my time away from him had prepared me for this moment. Heart pounding, sweating dripping down my back, I followed up my first question by asking another. "So, what made you hurt Mummy the way you did all those years?" *Forward much, Lovern? I chastised myself. Way to ease your way into it.*

"What do you mean?" he asked.

I repeated myself, making sure to emphasize each word.

He was silent for a moment but when he finally spoke, his tone was calm and measured. "Well, you see, as an intellectual, I have to navigate life under different terms while doing my best with things overall. You know?"

Huh? His words seemed to go around the world and back again without making any sense. The nonsensical response angered me because it came off as deflective.

"That all doesn't make sense. So again, what made you hurt Mummy the way you have all these years?" At this point, I had lost all of my inhibition and was ready to give him a piece of my mind if he came back with more rubbish.

"You know, your mother was to blame for most of that, right?" he said.

Nope. He didn't just say what I thought he did...right? Are you kidding me?

Before I could say anything else, he got distracted by his friend's car pulling up and immediately walked away from me to converse with him. I was left standing there sickened, and again feeling sorry for Lloydie. It was disgusting that he would try to blame anyone but himself for any of what he imposed on his wife and our family.

A few moments later, it registered that I had a voice Lloydie actually tolerated. I had come to him with a combative set of questions, and he listened and responded to me without retaliating! This was definitely another win for me. As long as I was around, I would use my tolerated voice to protect our mother.

***

Over the next two years I fell back into island life, becoming part of the working class of Trinidad. I took a couple of jobs that didn't last long before landing a job as a bank teller at a popular credit union. I worked there for over a year and loved it, especially because my income was quite high for a 20-year-old with very few financial responsibilities. Lloydie loved it too, because I was a professional working woman who made enough money to pay a couple of bills in the household. I sensed his pride every day when I left for work.

That year I heard that the acclaimed U.S. recording artist, Luther Vandross, was going to be in town. I knew how much Mummy and Lloydie loved his music. I told Mummy that I wanted to treat them to a night out with dinner, show tickets, and a car service that would chauffeur them to Luther's Valentine's Day show.

"Oh yes!" She responded, her eyes lighting up with excitement. "But, ask your father. He has to give the okay."

When I asked him that afternoon, that smirk came across his face again as he answered. "Okay, sure, big time working woman," he said sarcastically.

What he didn't understand was that I wasn't trying to come across as a big spender by sending them to this concert. I simply wanted the opportunity to see Mummy and Lloydie in love once again. I wanted to see him show her physical affection because I knew the spark between them was still there. I had seen it more than a few times growing up, but never consistently. I just wanted to play Cupid and fix my parents up on a date. This was another instance of living in the States rubbing off on me; I had been exposed to even more possibilities of what love is and how it can be created.

The night of the big date played out like a Hollywood red carpet premiere for my mother. She wore a loosely fitted, cap sleeved, champagne-colored jumpsuit with strategically placed sequins. Her hair closely mirrored the popular Toni Braxton hairstyle and her makeup was flawless, finished with burgundy lipstick and clip-on diamond earrings. In my eyes, she was the image of perfection. Lloydie also looked dapper with a fresh touch up from the barber, soft black pants, a pale yellow shirt, and black dress shoes. As we waited for their car to arrive, I went over the itinerary for the evening. My mother's eyes gleamed with excitement at every detail. This night was for her, not him, but his love for her showed in his eyes exactly as I had hoped it would. When the car arrived, they left for their night out looking like royalty. I was ecstatic!

I waited up for them to return instead of going to sleep at my regular hour. When they did return, I was at the door like a mom waiting for her daughter to get home from her first date. They came in the front door, and from the expressions on their faces, I could tell it had been a successful outing. Mummy was still beaming and Lloydie immediately volunteered how amazing the night had been from beginning to end. As I hung on his every word as he told me about the date, Mummy occasionally interjected to confirm his details with "Yes, yes!" or "Oh, yes, that was nice." Once he was through he thanked me for the night out, which made my heart feel extremely full. It was a night to remember for all of us. In the weeks that followed, there were no physical assaults against Mummy and fewer verbal assaults than usual. Our home environment was relatively calm. It was about eighteen years too late to finally have peace in the house, but I wasn't complaining.

About six months later, the immigration paperwork my grandparents filled out was finally approved. That meant Mummy, Sean, Javan, and I had officially received permanent residency status in the States. To everyone's surprise, my father was ready to allow my Mummy to depart with us. I was thrilled that he seemed to be turning over a new leaf. *Could this really be happening?* I found myself continuously thinking. *Could her horror finally be coming to an end?* I believe Lloydie faced the fact that his power over Mummy was lessening given the presence of his grown children. We were not afraid of him anymore, and we always protected her. His bloodsport of a marriage wasn't what it used to be, and he seemed to be coming to terms with that.

On the day of our flight to the States, Lloydie accompanied us to the airport. This was going to be my brothers' and Mummy's first time on a plane. They were all smiling with nervous excitement. It was both a joyous day and the end of an era, as well as a super exciting transition for her and my brothers.

Lloydie and Mummy hugged and kissed briefly, and I saw him whisper some sweet nothings in her ear. I watched as they filled their last moments together on Trinidad soil with a love rarely seen during the course of their marriage. After their goodbyes were over Lloydie briefly hugged me and each of my brothers, and then the four of us unceremoniously departed.

CHAPTER 3:
Red Flagged Date Night

I spent the first couple months back in the States introducing Mummy and my younger brothers to things I had become acclimated to during my first set of years living with my grandparents. Things like using the public transportation systems, grocery shopping, and navigating the school system. Even though it was a happy time for us as four new American residents, our entire family suffered a blow when our beloved grandmother, Antia, suffered a series of heart attacks that ultimately took her away from us in November of 1998. The small, neat, soft spoken matriarch of our family was suddenly gone. Trying to understand how a sweet soul like hers could be gone so soon was hard on our entire family.

Shortly before Antia's passing, Aunt Claire was diagnosed with pancreatic cancer. This was another devastating blow to the family. She took after Antia in many ways including her mannerisms and the level of care she showed for everyone in her circle. I had spent many weekends at her house in my early years in Trinidad, and remembered the way she cared for her three girls, my cousins. She had the motherly ability to be both soft and stern, and know when her children needed each one. I also watched how firm and strong of an individual she could be, even toward her husband when the situation warranted it. That certainly was not the norm in my house, and I loved seeing it from her. She seemed to live her life with a balance of strength and tenderness. I admired her for that. Seeing her suffer from cancer was terribly hard. Her decline was fast and she passed away in March of 1999. Another beautiful soul taken far too soon.

I needed to move full speed ahead with personal goals to try to help quell the pain of so much loss in such a short period of time. I was not sure how to begin to verbalize the level of sadness I felt to anyone in the family. As a granddaughter and a niece in all of this, not someone closer to the deceased, I didn't feel as if my grief fit in.

I turned 21 in September of 1998, right after we left Trinidad. I was now two years behind my peers who had started college right after high school. I

Grandmother Antia and Aunt Claire

began to submit college applications, making sure to include the school I had dreamed of attending one day: Suffolk University.

For a long time, I had fantasized of becoming a lawyer. Suffolk was one of the top schools that could prepare me for that, but I was self conscious of being so far behind my peers and was not confident in pursuing a law degree that late in the game. I was accepted to Suffolk the following month and, instead of law, decided to pursue an Advertising and Marketing Degree as a full time night student. During my high school years, I had been part of an internship program called ADop. It turned out that I was very good at making marketing pitches, inheriting the "gift of gab" from Lloydie. I also genuinely enjoyed meeting and talking with new people, so this degree seemed like the perfect alternative. I felt especially comfortable changing my academic focus because I no longer felt the need to prosecute our father for everything he had done to Mummy. Locking him up and throwing away the key was not at the top of my to-do list anymore. Mummy was safe now.

My brothers, Mummy, and I started looking for an apartment of our own and I began working an entry level job as a junior secretary for the customer service department of Filene's Basement's corporate office in Downtown Boston. I thought I had it all together and was on a path to independence.

One of my duties at work was a daily visit to the floor where customer service representatives were located to drop off paperwork. During the first few months of this practice, there was a guy on that floor who seemed hell bent on catching my attention whenever I visited. He was about ten years my senior, but didn't look it to me. After months of flirtation whenever I walked by his desk, I finally gave in and gave him my phone number. It was that day that I also learned his name: Guy.

Guy and I started talking on the phone after work, and sometimes even before work, getting to know each other. The following week he asked me on a date, I said yes, and we made plans for a night out.

On the evening of our much-anticipated date, I waited in the living room by the window to see when he arrived. I did not want my family to meet Guy just yet because I didn't know how our chemistry would be in person. They knew I was going out for the evening, but didn't give too much detail. There was also so much happening within the family with Antia and Aunt Claire's passing, it did not seem right or respectful to introduce a new relationship into the mix.

I saw Guy pull up in an older model Volvo and thought, *Okay, the car kinda fits with his vibe. I can dig it.* From the living room window that looked out onto the street, I watched with the lights off as he came up the steps to the porch and approached the door. After he rang the bell, he smoothed his clothes out and waited for me to answer. Tons of butterflies fluttered around in my stomach as I walked to the door, trying to compose myself. This was going to be my first real date. I wore an above-the-knee, form-fitted, floral dress with spaghetti straps, medium-height heeled shoes, and demure silver jewelry. My hair had been freshly washed, dried, and spiral curled from a roller set. I was not a fan of makeup, so I didn't wear any. I felt super cute from head to toe!

I also smoothed my dress out one last time, took a deep breath, and opened the door. I stepped onto the first floor porch and said, "Hello!" with a big, wide smile.

I'll never forget the look on his face. There was no immediate verbal answer to my greeting, but his eyes said, *Wow!* After a few seconds, it seemed like he had recovered from his surprise well enough to say, "Well, hello yourself, Baby."

"Well aren't we forward...calling me Baby," I responded assertively.

"Why? Is someone else referring to you as that?" Guy asked with a smirk lining his lips.

"Of course not, I think it's cute. I just wasn't expecting it, is all. C'mon, let's go!" I excitedly grasped his hand and led him down the porch stairs to the car.

I felt *something* in that moment as we walked to his car but couldn't put my finger on it; I couldn't tell if it made me feel good, bad or indifferent. He had always referred to me by my first name and that term of endearment threw me off. I was so caught up in all the attention that he had been pouring my way, that I quickly dismissed whatever that feeling was and chalked it up to cultural differences. Maybe calling me "Baby" was an American thing that my Trini self was not hip to, since Guy was born in the States. I also felt a little bit bad for possibly coming off as standoffish and giving him a hard time for something so trivial in the first five minutes of our night out.

"I'm just messing with you," he said as we headed to the car. "Just glad I finally get to see you outside of work, especially when you look as amazing as you do right now."

This put me at ease. He guided me to the passenger side of the car where he opened my door so I could get in. When he walked around to his side, I remembered a scene from the movie *A Bronx Tale*. As a huge fan of crime dramas, I had watched this and other Italian gangster movies a million times. In this movie, Chazz Palminteri's character schools his young friend, an Italian teenage boy prepping to go out on his first date with an African American teenage girl, about the test he needs to perform to see if she's "a keeper." If you have already helped her get seated on the passenger side of the car, she should then hurry to reach over and open your driver's side door before you get a chance to do it yourself. In the movie, Chazz said it meant that she wasn't selfish. With this in mind, I hurriedly stretched over to Guy's side and opened his door for him. When he arrived at the driver's side of the car, he grabbed the door handle from the outside to finish opening it.

"Thank you. Aren't you thoughtful?" he mused as he sat down. I hoped that he had also seen the movie and knew there was a meaning behind the gesture. Before driving away from the front of the house, he complimented me a few more times on the way I looked. I thanked him, and we were off.

After parking the car in a garage in the city, we walked to a nearby Chinese restaurant in the Downtown Crossing area of Boston. The temperature was just right for walking on this early Spring evening. We held hands and walked together in stride. When we arrived at the restaurant the hostess seated us fairly quickly, then Guy excused himself to the bathroom. When he left the table, I thought to myself, *So this is what it feels like to be on a grown-up date?* When he returned we ordered our food and commenced talking and laughing as we waited.

After an appetizing dinner, we left the restaurant and headed in the opposite direction of where the car was parked. I asked him why, and he said, "I want to extend the evening if that's okay with you."

I agreed, wanting to see what else he had in store. We walked for a bit and came to a small flower shop. Bouquets stored in buckets spilled out of the small doorway onto the sidewalk. I commented on how beautiful they all looked as we approached, and he said, "What's your favorite color?"

"Purple," I replied.

He gestured with his right hand for me to slow our pace, and walked up to the flower shop attendant. "Excuse me," he asked, "can I please buy a purple rose for my lady?"

His lady? Roses actually come in purple? My mind was spinning with anticipation and I couldn't get over how romantic it all was! I grinned from ear to ear as he paid the attendant, took the rose, and handed it to me, standing inches away from my face. After thanking him, I put the flower up to my nose to inhale its sweet scent.

When I moved it away from my face, he leaned in and we shared our first kiss that sent chills up and down my spine. He held me so close, hands wrapped around my waist and caressing my back. His lips were impossibly soft and he smelled like vanilla and lavender. I was falling hard and fast for Guy. Before tonight, nobody had ever made me feel electric. Similar to domestic happiness, the only reference point I had for dates were TV shows. I couldn't believe I was having a TV-perfect date in real life!

When we finally unlocked our lips, my knees buckled a little. He noticed this and held me steady with a big smile on his face.

"You alright?" he asked.

I nodded yes, overcome with a giddiness and giggles. He let go of my waist and took my hand in his, and we continued our walk. We soon came to a busy intersection that crossed over to the Boston Commons. We strolled through the scenic park, people watching, talking, laughing, and stopping to kiss a few more times along the way. It all felt so very magical. After walking for so long, my heels started to hurt my feet. I was no stranger to walking in heels, but no pair has ever been made for a long stroll.

"I'd like to sit for a bit," I told Guy, not wanting to let on that my feet were sore. We found a nearby bench and he guided me onto it. He started to do the same, but halfway through doing so, something behind me caught his eye. He paused, staring, a very serious look on his face.

"Is everything all right?" I asked.

"It's fine, just this dude getting close here." He replied in a very concerned tone.

After he brought his concern to my attention, I too started watching as the man casually passed our bench. Guy said he thought the man was approaching to sit on the same bench as us. I thought it was odd that he would assume such a thing since it would be clear to anyone walking by that Guy and I were taking up most of the bench, but I brushed it off.

With a genuinely puzzled look on his face, Guy asked why I kept staring at the stranger walking off into the distance.

"I wasn't staring," I explained. "I only glanced at him a couple times after you brought him up."

"Oh okay…" he said as he got comfortable on the bench. I was now conscious that I shouldn't look in the direction of the man, but I couldn't help focusing on him.

The moment with the stranger ended so quickly that I barely had time to process just how weird it was. Plus, Guy distracted me by saying more kind and beautiful things like he had in the car in front of my house. It was like a switch had gone off inside of him for a few minutes, then back on again as he reverted to his charming self. He took both my hands in his, gently gliding his thumb back and forth across the back of my hand.

"I wish tonight didn't have to end," he cooed into my ear. "I love hearing you talk. When your Trinidadian accent comes through, it's beautiful. I could listen to you all night. I am so happy you gave me a chance. I didn't think you would." I was captivated hearing him talk like this. Whatever mixed feelings I had in prior moments were now a distant memory.

A little while later, I told him I felt a little cold even though I was already wearing the cardigan I had brought along. He gave me his light jacket to wear, and we both decided it was time to head back to the car so he could bring me home. We walked back to the garage and then drove back to my house.

After we pulled up in front of the house, we sat in his car for a while. "All That I Can Say" by Mary J. Blige played quietly on the radio. He gently passed the back of his hand across my cheek, finally letting it rest softly in the corner of my neck, which prompted us to kiss passionately a few more times. As we prepared to say our last goodbye, I saw out the corner of my eye that someone was peeping from the living room window. They stood in the same spot I had been earlier that night to watch Guy as he came up the walk. Peering a little harder, I saw that it was Mummy. That was the cue I needed to get inside to spill date details.

Guy exited the car, came around to open my door, and let me out. He walked me to the front gate where we hugged one more time. As I opened the front door to enter the house, I glanced back to see him waiting for me to get inside with a huge smile on his face. I waved to him and then closed the door behind me. I barely heard him whisper, "Goodnight, beautiful" before the door shut all the way. It was the end of a perfect first date.

Mummy, the Peeping Tomtress, met me just inside the door and asked how the night had gone.

"You have the look of love in your eyes!" she exclaimed before I could answer. That made me chuckle because she read me like an open book. We walked into our shared bedroom and I gave an overview of the night. She was impressed by all of his romanticisms, exclaiming "Papayo!" several times as I talked. This exclamation was Trinidadian slang for "Well, excuse me!" and was usually used in exciting situations like this one.

"The next time he comes to pick you up, you must bring him in to meet your grandfather," Mummy said when I was finished. I agreed. At this point, I was smitten with Guy and certain the relationship was headed somewhere positive.

***

Mummy had been adjusting well to her new life and was diligently seeking a job. Unfortunately, the job market was slim for someone with an elementary school education and only household work as experience. I started to help the effort by looking at online job boards, and came upon a kitchen position at a rehab hospital in Boston. I told her the position would be great as a starter job, and that she could potentially move on from after she got her foot in the door.

"Who, me?" she asked in disbelief. "You think a hospital will hire me? Oh Lord."

I laughed uncomfortably at this. Not because of what she said, but how she said it. Mummy was always the master of self deprecation with a humorous tone. For example, when we lived in Trinidad and went on visits to see her siblings, they would express worry about her plight with Lloydie and she would somehow find a way to make light of the situation. Before long, everyone in her presence would be laughing along with her. I never understood how she turned her pain into a laughing matter, but laughed along with her because she made it funny.

We sat together as I helped her make a gleaming resume that screamed "amazing, hard worker with tons of life experience." She applied and about a week later, she got a call for an interview. She came home hired! She started off on a per-diem schedule, but wasn't long before she was hired as a permanent employee. Her foot was in the door and I was excited for her big step toward her independence.

As she got settled into the position, she started picking up more shifts until she was working a full time schedule. This meant the leisure time she usually used to call Lloydie dwindled more and more. After coming home from a double shift, she would sometimes step out and walk to the corner store that sold a specific long distance phone calling card that allowed her to talk to him for up to fifteen minutes. While she would also call my older siblings back in Trinidad, the main use of these cards was dedicated to chatting with Lloydie every single day. I began to get frustrated with her, because no matter how tired she was from working, it seemed like there was a mandated time to check in with him that she could not miss. Here she was, thousands of miles away from him, still feeling obligated to let him control her time. I let her know how much I disapproved of this practice, but she brushed it off as no big deal. After a few months of this, I overheard her making stern comments while she talked on the phone with him one evening.

"So you're telling me that they're lying?" she asked, referring to our neighbors in Trinidad. "So you don't have another woman sleeping in our house with you? I know you're lying to me." I was caught up in the drama, but still took a moment to admire her newfound brazen boldness. Lloydie seemed to appease her with an explanation that the neighbors were simply making up stories. When she hung up the phone, I asked her why she was accepting what we both knew were lies. She had no response.

Bronson confirmed the truth to me when I called him to ask him about it. Lloydie had started seeing another woman who made frequent visits to the house, but it wasn't something Bronson wanted to tell Mummy because he knew it would upset her. After all the years of torture Lloydie inflicted on Mummy, he had the nerve to move another woman into the house almost as

soon as we had left the island. He and Mummy were still married! Even as I seethed over the matter, the logical part of me did some deducing. It started to make sense why he had finally let our mother board a plane and finally leave his sight. In part, it must have been because this other woman was lurking in the shadows.

With no family pictures, Lovern organized this one during Lloydie's brief visit in the States with, Javan, their Mummy and Sean

I sat Mummy down and told her that she needed to let him be and focus on being her best self. What I did not understand was that my argument was competing with years and years of emotional brainwashing, which was still happening even though Lloydie was nowhere in sight. Mummy needed more time before the fog that had infected her brain all those years would begin to clear.

About a month later, Mummy announced that Lloydie was coming to visit us in the States for a month. I immediately thought, Why? I also felt a little conflicted; while I had no respect for him carrying on this blatant affair, I did want him to see that we were all thriving without him.

Lloydie arrived in Boston in the early Spring of 1999 for a three-week stay. Mummy, Sean, and Javan were delighted. I mustered up enough emotion to be respectful and tolerant of his presence, but I was not excited to see him.

One Sunday morning while he was visiting, I was up early baking mac and cheese as my contribution to Sunday lunch. Lloydie came into the kitchen and sat down. We exchanged pleasantries and then were quiet as I continued to bustle from countertop to stove, getting the dish ready to go into the oven.

After a while he asked, "So, you don't use block cheese for your pie?" He was referring to a Trinidadian dish somewhat similar American mac and cheese. I responded politely, explaining the differences in the two dishes and why I personally used a variety of shredded cheese in my version. He seemed very interested and impressed by it all. Just then my grandfather, who happened to be up early as well that morning, entered the kitchen to say good morning to us. The men began to engage in banter and eventually walked away toward the front door while I finished cooking.

The mac and cheese exchange was now the second conversation Lloydie and I had ever had, and I unexpectedly found myself a little sad at the exchange's abrupt end. I yearned for a normal father-daughter relationship with him, but could never let go of the monster that I knew existed in him. When his visit was over and he departed for Trinidad I was left with a huge pile of conflicting emotions, but none of them amounted to me wishing he would return.

CHAPTER 4:
Ice Cream

During Lloydie's stay, I chose not to introduce him to Guy. Given my complicated relationship with my father, I asked Guy to respect that Lloydie would be in town and that I was not ready for the two of them to meet. He respected my wishes and stayed away from the house, although we still got to see each other during the work day.

Guy was the first person I had truly confided in about the love-hate relationship I had with Lloydie, as well as the abuse my siblings and mother had faced growing up. I told Guy I was determined never to end up in a relationship like the one my parents had. He listened to me intently, comforted me when the tears flowed, and reassured me that I was safe. He let me unload my horrible childhood memories as well as my sadness around the recent passing of my aunt and grandmother. I trusted him with my grief.

After my father traveled back to Trinidad, Guy resumed coming by the house to pick me up. Before our next date, I met him outside the house and asked him to come and officially meet Pappy and Mummy. He happily obliged.

"This must be the real thing if I'm getting to meet Mummy and G'pop tuh-day!" he exclaimed jokingly.

"Just be your usual, charming self and it'll continue to be the real thing," I told him through my laughter.

We entered through the front door and were met by my grandfather in the hallway. Pappy's facial expression was not a pleasant one at the first sighting of Guy.

"Nice to meet you, sir," Guy said nervously.

"Hello," Pappy responded, still with a cross look on his face. "Listen. When you meet a girl's family, you should always extend a firm handshake to the men at the house. That's a sign of respect!"

Guy chuckled apprehensively, then extended his right hand to do as he had been instructed. Pappy extended his hand in return, and they shook hands for the longest few seconds in the world. When the exchange finished

Pappy turned away from us and walked into the kitchen, giving no indication that he wanted us to follow him. His not-so-welcoming demeanor toward Guy was to be expected, I guessed. He was still mourning the loss of his beloved wife and daughter. I had just wanted to show him respect by letting him know who I was with when I wasn't at the house, school, or work, and now I had.

Mummy, who had just witnessed the cold exchange, passed Pappy as he entered the kitchen on her way to meet us in the hallway. She greeted Guy and extended her hand to him. He returned the handshake with a greeting, addressing her as Mummy. After the brief pleasantries, she wished us well and we were off. I was relieved that at least a couple of family members had met him.

As we drove away, Guy told me why he didn't mind what had just transpired. I was pleasantly surprised by the way he justified the odd interaction with Pappy. He explained that my grandfather had a smart, beautiful granddaughter; if Pappy had liked Guy too much off the bat, Guy would question whether my grandfather really cared about my safety around a virtual stranger. I thought this was a fair and mature interpretation.

Going out for ice cream soon became one of our more frequent dates. As a lover of most sweets, I looked forward to the delicious snack as much as I looked forward to spending time with him.

When we went out together Guy talked here and there about his life, but never in depth. Whenever I pressed him to scratch the surface, he clammed up or quickly turned the conversation back to me. I liked the attention but in reality, my gut should have been yelling at things at me like, *Lovern, this is not normal! Who are his people? Why haven't you met them yet? Why haven't you been to his place yet? How come he always comes to you?* I assumed he was not close to his family, maybe

During one of our many ice-cream dates

embarrassed by them or by where he lived. Like me, he probably wasn't eager to share parts of his past yet, and probably didn't have too many friends outside of work. These were all fair explanations, but not ones that he himself had given. In reality, this behavior should have been a huge red flag to me.

I did not yet understand that the information I was pouring out to him was being used to study and dissect my personality. The confident, high achieving, self-assured social butterfly he had met at the office was now showing vulnerability and weakness about her past. The girl who had confessed that she was always changing and adapting to situations to gain the admiration of others was almost ready to be tamed to his liking. I was a challenge he was ready to tackle head on.

Red Flags / Warning Signs:

1. *Extreme jealousy and possessiveness*
2. *Unpredictable, bad temper*
3. *Cruelty to animals/pets*
4. *Verbal abuse*
5. *Antiquated beliefs about roles of women and men in relationships*
6. *Forced sex or disregard of partner's unwillingness to have sex*
7. *Blaming the victim for anything bad that happens, never takes accountability*
8. *Sabotage or obstruction of the victim's ability to work or attend school*
9. *Controls all the finances*
10. *Accusations of the victim flirting with others or cheating*
11. *Control of what you wear and how you act*
12. *Demeaning you - either privately or publicly*
13. *Harassment at work*
14. *Gaslighting - often has you questioning your own perception of reality*

Source: *National Coalition Against Domestic Violence - https://ncadv.org/ signs-of-abuse*

CHAPTER 5:
The Change

Later that year, I had switched jobs and was in my third month working as a National Business Development Representative for a venture leasing company. Guy was laid off from the job where he and I had met, but we both looked at it as time he could take to regroup and look for another opportunity. Things weren't ideal, but we were happy.

One weekday morning, I started suffering from really bad allergies. It felt like an awful cold: sneezing, congestion, lethargy, and the first time I had experienced watery and itchy eyes. I was down for the count and had no energy to rise and get dressed for work, so after the third time hitting the snooze button, I called the office to let them know I would be taking a sick day and went back to bed.

About ten minutes later, my cell phone rang. I saw it was Guy calling and answered happily. With no reciprocation to my greeting, he asked irately, "Why aren't you at work? I called your desk, you didn't answer and when I dialed out to the receptionist, she said you weren't in today. Why are you at home?"

"Well, I'm actually feeling really sick this morning. Are you gonna come bring me some chicken soup?" I said playfully.

"Chicken soup?" he responded in disgust before abruptly hanging up the phone.

Shocked, I looked at my phone screen to see that he really had hung up on me. A message popped up that I had missed a few calls from him while I was asleep since the ringer had been on vibrate. I thought, *Well, I guess he does have a right to be upset.* Guy called me every morning before I left the house, while on my way to work, and soon after I got to my desk. I hadn't answered any of our usual calls. I decided his rude attitude stemmed from worry since he hadn't heard from me that morning.

There were times I could have done without some of the calls while I got ready for work or headed into the office, but I always felt obligated to take them. I never wanted him to think I was brushing him off or not welcoming his attention. In hindsight, the constant phone calls were him checking up on me to see where I was every minute of the day, a common way abusers keep track of their victims.

About fifteen minutes after his irate phone call, the doorbell rang. I wondered who it could be since everyone on all three floors of the house had already left for work or school. I dragged myself out of bed and looked through the peephole at the front door. It was Guy.

I was excited he had decided to come by and thought he must have realized he was wrong for being so curt with me earlier. I opened the door, expecting a hug or some other affectionate greeting. Instead, I was met with a look of fury as he hastily brushed past me into the house. Confused, I closed the door and followed him into my bedroom where I could hear him shuffling around and knocking things about. I entered the room and sat at the foot of the bed in dismay as he talked angrily to himself about me in third person as he continued to rifle through my belongings.

"So, Lovern thinks she's smarter than everybody, huh? She thinks she can mess around on me and I wouldn't ever find out, huh?"

"Mess around on who?" I asked in confusion. "What in the world are you talking about?"

He ignored me and continued to mumble while frantically pulling back my sheets on one side of the bed, looking under the bed frame, pulling out my chest of drawers to poke around its contents, suspiciously peeking through my windows, and rummaging through my closet. I watched as he moved about, feeling like I was in my very own episode of *The Twilight Zone* or watching a real life Dr. Jekyll and Mr. Hyde transformation. The random onslaught of aggression scared me. I wasn't sure what to do except reassure him over and over that I had not had any guests that morning.

"I would never mess around on you. I want you and only you! You know that!" The more I sought to affirm this, the angrier he got.

After about two minutes of this paranoid, accusatory behavior, he stood over me, red in the face with hate in his eyes.

"I knew you were too good to be true!" he yelled. He slapped me across the face so hard that my entire body shook. I saw stars as I tried to steady myself from the blow. After a few seconds my eyes refocused on the image of him leaving the room in haste.

I had never been slapped before. Not even by my father, who dished out blows like they were blessings on a Sunday morning. The feeling was a combination of sharp pain and an intense stinging sensation. I heard the front door slam shut, indicating that Guy had left the house. I continued to sit at the edge of the bed, shocked by what had just transpired. I held my face to try and ease the pain. Uncontrollable tears began streaming down my cheeks as I cried audibly.

After a few minutes, I put on my robe and headed out onto the front porch to see if he was still outside hanging around in his car. He wasn't. I decided to sit on one of the chairs to catch my breath and try to make sense of it all. What had I done wrong to trigger this drastic, angry behavior in my usually caring partner? What could I have done to prevent the situation? Well, I thought, *maybe I should have checked in with him and had my ringer on to not miss his calls. I guess it really was my fault?*

After about five minutes of self doubt and questioning my actions, I caught myself. The truth was that I had not lied to him and there were zero reasons for him to have acted the way he did. At that moment, I made the decision to be done with Guy. It wasn't like we had any kids together, nor were we married. There was nothing tying us together and I was not willing to forgive and forget, even if he came back later with an apology.

I remembered the life my mother had lived with Lloydie. I knew a man beating on his partner in the name of love was wrong, but had never heard the terms "domestic violence" or "abuse" before. All I understood that morning was that Guy had treated me like my father had treated my mother. The difference to me was that I was strong and wouldn't accept that treatment going forward. Not for promises of love, attention, or any other incentive.

Now resolute, I went back inside. My face was swollen and my feelings and pride were hurt. I knew my family members would be home later on, and I couldn't let them see me in the state that I was in. I also couldn't show up to work with any sort of lingering bruise that would warrant questions being asked. To help with the swelling, I put some ice cubes in a thin T-shirt and pressed the makeshift ice pack gently against my cheek. The cold hurt my face on contact, but I had to work through the pain if I wanted any result from the TV remedy I had seen so many times. I took myself to bed, the ice pack affixed to my cheek, and fell asleep crying.

A couple of hours later, I woke up feeling even more confident that washing my hands of Guy was the right thing to do. I decided that I would take the weekend trip to New York that I had begun thinking about a few months prior. It had been my intention to eventually ask Guy if he would accompany me, but between him being laid off and now this incident, that was no longer on the table. I needed time to decompress, and this adventure was just what I needed to remove him from my thoughts.

The Friday morning of my departure for New York arrived. As I got myself together to leave, I asked Mummy and my brothers to not disclose where I was headed in the event that Guy came by looking for me. I told them we were through and I didn't want to see him again. They wanted to know the sordid details of the sudden breakup, but I remained tight lipped. Later that morning, I hopped on one of the Chinese bus lines that departed hourly to take people on the four-hour trip to New York from Boston.

When I arrived in Brooklyn I rented a motel room, had lunch, and gave my hair some TLC at a nearby salon. The hairstylist I was paired with asked what brought me to Brooklyn as she massaged my crown during the soothing wash process.

"I just broke up with my boyfriend back in Boston," I said confidently. "This trip is a reaffirmation of self!" Too ashamed of the details of the break-up, I didn't explain further. She loved the idea and agreed that I needed this time for me.

I wrapped up the visit with a head full of bouncy curls and headed back to the motel where I changed clothes and hit the streets to shop and grab dinner. By the end of the first day, I was still thinking about Guy here and there, but I'd turned off my cell phone to conserve minutes and so that I wouldn't hear from him if he tried calling.

I ventured into Manhattan the next day to explore, and had a wonderful day. I slept in on Sunday and got up in time to check out from the motel and catch the bus that would get me back to Boston by 6pm that evening, giving me plenty of time to get ready for work the next day. This had been my first solo trip anywhere, and while nothing about it was eventful, it made me feel empowered and sure of myself. I had put on my big girl panties for the first time and it felt good!

When I arrived home, my nineteen-year-old brother Sean was on the front porch. He had a weird look of excitement mixed with concern on his face. I walked to the top of the porch stairs where he stood.

"What'd you bring for me from your trip?" he asked.

"Zero, zilch, and nada, player. But what's wrong?"

"Nothing," he said, but his expression grew even more bothered. I asked him why that was and he replied, "Guy came by here looking for you earlier today and dropped something off. It's in your bedroom."

"Were you the only one who talked with him? You didn't tell him where I was, did you?" I asked in a panicked tone.

"Nah, nah. You asked me not to tell him, didn't you? He only spoke to me, but real talk, I'm kinda mad you ain't brought nothing back for me after my secrecy services," he said sarcastically.

I dug into my purse, searching for a $10 or $20 bill as a reward to him for his "services". As I did so, he asked way too many questions."Yo, did Guy hit you or something? Why is he trying so hard to see you? And why'd you run off to New York like that, as if you were on the run?"

With my head down, continuing to rummage through my bag for money, I wondered how in the world his suspicions were so spot on. The idea that he had even suspected anything meant Guy might have said something incriminating when he came by. Finally I found money and raised it triumphantly in my fist.

"You are crazy if you think I would let anybody put their hands on me," I said as I extended the money to him. "Here, take this $20 for your time, sir, and get that thought outta your head. I just needed some time away is all. I'm over him. That's it." I headed inside, my shopping bag from the trip on my forearm. My thoughts were still consumed with what Guy might have said to him earlier that day.

I walked into my bedroom and found two dozen purple roses—I counted—in a beautiful glass vase on top of my dresser. They were strikingly gorgeous and I was mesmerized by the sight of them. If he was trying to speak to me without being present or making a statement, it was working.

A card peeked through the top middle of the beautiful arrangement, which I moved closer to read. *I'm sorry. I miss you. I'm worried. I love you. Please call me back. Love, Guy.*

"Please call me back"? So he had been calling. I turned on my phone and checked my voicemail. I listened to seven messages from him. Each message sounded intense, sincere, and deeply apologetic. He said he hated what he did to me and professed how much he loved me. He confessed that the thought of me being with someone else drove him crazy. He begged for one more chance to make it up to me.

After hearing all the messages and admiring the flowers a bit longer, almost every piece of self assurance I had picked up in New York was erased. I began to question myself. *I mean, it was just a slap, right?* I decided that equating one tiny slap with the level of abuse my mother had endured was ridiculous. I needed to take some of the blame for my part in this. Plus, Guy had gone to great lengths to apologize. The way I looked at it was, my father never took accountability for his actions, let alone took elaborate steps to say he was sorry. I surmised that I needed to stop being so prideful and at least hear him out, so I called him.

Guy's phone rang only once before he answered my call. He sounded relieved to hear from me. He immediately showered me with excited apologies. When I could get a word in, I apologized for overreacting. I gushed over the flowers and told him I'd missed him too, referring to the note attached to the bouquet.

He asked me where I had disappeared that weekend. I opened up about my trip as well as things I had done while there. As I rambled on about the fun I had in New York, he abruptly cut me off.

"You meet up with any guys there? Or were you talking to any of your guy friends on the phone, seeing as you weren't talking to me?"

I reassured him I hadn't, but also wasn't in the mood not to be trusted after all our drama that week. He immediately reigned himself in from that line of questioning, apologized, and instead asked when the next time was that we could get together because he had a special overnight date planned for us. I told him the following Friday would work. Just like that, his apology was accepted.

Guy's manipulation tactics were on full display, but I didn't see them. I was appeased by the gift and the over-apologizing. I took partial blame for something I did not do and let him off the hook with no accountability whatsoever. I allowed him to dangle a future date and promises of more good times in front of me. Guy was testing me, and after that phone call, knew he could move on to the next level of control.

I finished up the phone call as Mummy entered the room and welcomed me back from the trip. She had just showered and wore a look of concern along with her robe. As she applied lotion to her arms, she asked why Guy had come by earlier with flowers. I told her that this was the way American men apologized after having simple arguments with their girlfriends. I told her we had just made up on the phone, everything was good now, and I was so happy to have a guy like him. By the end of the conversation her look of concern lessened and she seemed happy that I was happy. As I put my head to the pillow that night, I wondered if I had done enough to convince my family that all was well.

CYCLE OF ABUSE

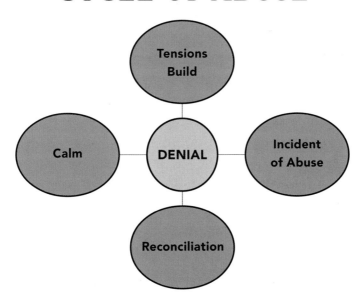

The Cycle of Abuse involves four stages:

1. *Building tension. Abusive partners often lash out in response to external stressors. Anything can fuel tension: family issues, trouble at work, physical illness, fatigue.*

2. *An incident of abuse. The abuser eventually releases this tension on others, attempting to regain power by establishing control.*

3. *Reconciliation. After the incident of abuse, tension gradually begins to fade. In an attempt to move past the abuse, the abuser often uses kindness, gifts, and loving gestures to usher in a "honeymoon" stage.*

4. *Calm. To maintain peace and harmony, both parties generally have to come up with some sort of explanation or justification for the abuse.*

Source: *https://www.healthline.com/health/relationships/cycle-of-abuse#the-cycle*

CHAPTER 6:
The Real Beginning

As it relates to abuse, I often hear people question what kind of person "lets themselves fall into" or "stay in" these types of relationships. From folks on the outside looking in, a common argument when referring to victims is, "That could never be me! I'm too strong and independent for anybody to ever think of putting their hands on me!" Before meeting him, I considered myself a smart, strong, and independent person, too. I thought I had groomed myself to be the opposite of my mother, yet somehow, here I was. I justified what I thought to be a small amount of abuse by rationalizing that it was nothing like the severe beatings Lloydie had regularly given Mummy. I didn't understand that there were many more comparisons between my parents and my relationship with Guy than what I allowed myself to see. I thought I could take control at any given point, but I was lying to myself. The truth was, I had lost control a long time ago and missed tons of red flags. I was in over my head against a skilled abuser.

In many cases, victims are targeted by abusers for their specific strengths, and then those strengths are used against them. A strong person in a healthy relationship creates a balance. In a toxic relationship, power and control are unbalanced from the beginning. The abuser can take any of the following strengths and manipulate them into weaknesses:

- Puts the needs of others before their own.
- Is faithful and trustworthy.
- Takes responsibility for themselves and those around them.
- Is generous to a fault—giving more than they take and doing it with pleasure.
- Is kind and compassionate. Very empathetic.
- Pick up on tone and body language, and adjust their approach accordingly.
- Will forgive endlessly.
- Will endure the attacks of their partner, believing this is not their "real" personality.

- Is courageous and resourceful.
- Is loyal and doesn't desire revenge, just wants to be treated with respect.

***

Early in the week, before our scheduled overnight date, Guy surprised me at work. He called to say he was downstairs ready to take me out to lunch because he couldn't wait until Friday to see me. I loved the initiative he took to show up like that, and definitely felt like love was in the air again. Even though I had not mentioned too much about him, my two close girlfriends at work could tell I was really smitten with Guy. That day I told them I would be going out to lunch with him and instead of our typical group walk to the nearby Il Giardino Cafe.

My office was on the second floor of the building, but I chose to take the stairs to get down to the lobby since the elevator was an impossibly slow choice for such a thrilling occasion. I opened the first floor door and there he was. I ran over and embraced him. He kissed me with a fierce intensity that showed how much he had missed me. Our embrace was interrupted by the dinging sound of the elevator, alerting us that someone was about to exit into the lobby. We pulled apart as the elevator doors opened, revealing my colleagues heading to lunch. They would finally get to meet the guy who was making their girl smile a little extra hard these days.

"So, this is him, huh?" one of them said, both then erupting into school-girl-like giggles. I could see that Guy loved the attention as I introduced them. After exchanging pleasantries, the girls went on their way and Guy and I headed to his car where he already had take-out lunch waiting for me. We drove to a nearby spot along the scenic riverway to sit in the car and reconnect. The mood was romantic and the short date built up the anticipation of seeing each other later that week. I still didn't know where he was going to take me; it was a surprise.

We had not slept together yet, and I knew this date would most likely lead to taking our relationship to the next level. I thought we had had our first and last rift, which I sensed was at least a small part of how adult relationships were supposed to go. The difference to me was that I believed I had a handle on it all going forward.

That Friday, he picked me up at my house as usual. We drove to a beautiful hotel on the South Shore. After checking in, we settled into the swanky room. It was even equipped with a jacuzzi tub covered in rose petals, something Guy had clearly arranged ahead of time. He sat me down on the bed next to him and presented me with a small Victoria's Secret gift bag.

"This is for you, Baby. I hope you like it," he said with a mischievous grin.

I peered inside and saw an off-white mini nightgown made of silk and lace. It was a very sexy negligee and the most luxurious nightgown I had ever seen. I gushed at his gift, gleefully exclaiming, "Thank you, Baby! I take it that you wanna see me in this, don't you?"

Guy smiled and nodded his head in enthusiastic agreement. This prompted me to scurry off to the bathroom to change into it.

From the bathroom, I heard him turn some Carl Thomas R&B music. I love good music and this was one of my favorite artists. As I draped myself in the luxurious fabric, I felt love all over me. Our miscommunication had led to an unfortunate chain of events, but we were good now and I was where I needed to be. I loved that I was finally experiencing a grown up kind of love.

I stepped out of the bathroom full of confidence. His eyes widened and brightened as he motioned for me to come closer to him, standing up to meet me halfway across the room. Upon connecting, we entered each other's arms. I melted into him as he kissed me passionately. His arms encased my body and I got lost in his lips. His fingers ran up and down my back, squeezed my shoulders gently, and glided to the back of my neck where they caressed the base of my curled hairline.

He was much more versed in the area of intimacy and it showed. He took his time exploring every part of me as we made love. Let's just say I learned a lot that night. When the pleasure and beauty were over, he laid next to me and stared lovingly in my direction under the dim light of the bedside lamp.

After a while, he said he wanted to run me a bath which sounded good to me. He got up and headed to the bathroom. Minutes later, he ushered me to join him once the tub had filled. I rolled up a towel to use as a makeshift pillow behind my head, pinned my head full of curls up nice and tight so they wouldn't get wet, and stepped into the warm, bubble-filled water. Once I was submerged, Guy sat on the opposite side and rubbed my feet using the foam of the bubbles and some of the rose petals. *This feels like a dream*, I thought as I closed my eyes and laid my head back against the towel. I was so very relaxed and completely in the moment.

I opened my eyes briefly to see that he was looking at me, both with love and distrust in his eyes. "So," he asked nonchalantly as our eyes connected, "who else have you had sex like that with before?"

The question came out of nowhere and my gut reaction was to laugh out loud. However, I soon realized he wasn't laughing along with me. His face looked overcome with even more distrust and disgust.

"Are you serious?" I responded. "You're not serious. You can't be."

"I am very serious, actually. Did you have sex like that with someone else when you ventured down to New York to give up on us?" His tone was devilish even though his voice stayed steady. He was turning red in the face, a now-familiar look that I knew meant trouble.

I knew immediately that I had to choose my response carefully in order for things to remain calm. I explained to him that I had never had an experience like the one we just had, that it all was like a dream and I had most definitely not been with anyone in New York. I further explained that it had been insanely hard trying to get over him in one weekend, and I was immensely happy to come home and find out he had been thinking about me too. I worked hard to deliver the truth so that he would believe me. I could tell my words weren't doing much to change his demeanor. I needed to turn this around, reign in the craziness that seemed to be taking place before my very eyes, *again*. I needed to reject the suspicion and lack of trust he was hurling at me.

"Was that the reason for this getaway tonight?" I asked sternly. "To show me how good I had it with you, then turn around and shame me for almost tossing it away?" He didn't answer but his expression grew more sinister. "Look, this is crazy! We made up so beautifully and I'm here with you!

I love you and only you! For you to suggest otherwise is insane and I'm offended, Guy. I thought we moved past this!"

I stood up from the tub and stormed into the bedroom, grabbing a towel on the way. I didn't even care that I was soaking wet and splashing water everywhere. I plopped down on the edge of the bed and started hastily drying myself off. I grabbed a bottle of lotion from my overnight bag since the hotel's tiny bottles were never enough for me, and started my usual after-shower moisturizing routine.

More than a few minutes passed and Guy did not emerge from the bathroom. Was he still red in the face? Did I make him more angry by storming off? Was he going to come out and slap me in retaliation for raising my voice at him? Should I get dressed and leave before he came out? If I did, how would I get home? As these thoughts ran through my head, I heard splashing water in the bathroom. It sounded like he had risen from the tub. A few minutes later he appeared in the bathroom doorway with a towel around his waist. He stood there with his shoulder propped against the wall, arms folded across his chest, staring at me as I finished up my lotion process.

"Look, I was just playing in there, okay? I didn't mean to come at you like that. I love you, and I know you love me too, baby girl. I just don't wanna lose you and it really paralyzed me when I thought I did. I wanted to show you that tonight and hope I didn't mess that up."

I teared up as he spoke and started feeling a little guilty. I had caused his mistrust to begin with by running off to New York the way I had, and now I needed to fix it. I got out of the bed, walked over to where he stood, and hugged him.

"I am very sorry, Babe. I will never run off like that again. You have me completely, and I promise you that I'm not going anywhere."

With that, he allowed me to lead him back to the bed where we made more sweet love. When it was over and he lay asleep next to me, I thought about how much more grateful I needed to be to have him as a boyfriend going forward. I needed to stop paying attention to the little mishaps here and there.

Emotional Abuse may begin suddenly. Some abusers may start out behaving normally and then begin abuse after a relationship is established. Some abusers may purposefully give a lot of love and attention, including compliments and requests to see you, in the beginning of a relationship. Often, the abuser tries to make the other person feel strongly bonded to them, as though it is the two of them "against the world."

Over time, abusers begin to insult or threaten their victims and begin controlling different parts of their lives. When this change in behavior happens, it can leave victims feeling shocked and confused. You may feel embarrassed or foolish for getting into the relationship.

<u>Examples of Emotional Abuse:</u>
- *Prevents or discourages you from seeing friends or family*
- *Tries to stop you from going to work or school*
- *Acts very jealous, including constantly accusing you of cheating*
- *Threatens to hurt you, people you care about, or pets*
- *Threatens to harm himself or herself when upset with you*
- *Says things like, "If I can't have you, then no one can"*
- *Decides things for you that you should decide (like what to wear or eat)*
- *Gaslight you by denying an event ever happened OR*
- *Call you crazy or overly sensitive*

***Source:** https://www.womenshealth.gov/relationships-and-safety/other-types/emotional-and-verbal-abuse*

TRADITIONAL GENDER STEREOTYPES

FEMININE	MASCULINE
✧ Not Aggressive	✧ Aggressive
✧ Dependent	✧ Independent
✧ Submissive	✧ Dominant
✧ Caretaker	✧ Not Nurturing
✧ Emotional	✧ Logical
✧ Cries a Lot	✧ Does Not Cry

***Source:** https://scalar.usc.edu/works/index-2/media/traditional-gender-stereotypes*

CHAPTER 7:
This Is Where It's At

I became more in tune with what it took to please Guy in the weeks that followed. I wanted to make him just as happy as he had made me. I see now that this was a twisted way of thinking, but at the time it felt like reality.

I found that conversations with male friends, whether in person or over the phone, should drop to zero. Guy questioned each relationship with menacing looks or snide remarks like, "Why do you need to talk to him? You know he just wants to get in your pants, right?" I knew this was not the case with my long time friends, but out of respect for his feelings and our relationship, I curbed communications with them.

Long phone calls or extended meet ups with girlfriends were also met with scrutiny. He believed they were always devising plans to hook me up with some other man, so I promised not to see most of them as well.

My family members were no exception as Guy continued to isolate me. At this point I was living with Sean, Javan, and Mummy in our own first floor apartment walking distance from the JFK Train Station. Even though my family was on the outside looking in, they had begun to see that things weren't as flowery and happy-go-lucky as I tried to make them think. I had gotten over the hurt they knew of, but they were still dwelling on the purple bouquet of apology flowers. They also began to see a change in my habits; friends weren't stopping by and I wasn't venturing out as much. My social life was suddenly all Guy, all the time.

One night, Guy said he wanted to take me to a hot club in the Downtown Boston area. I was excited to get prettied up for him and dance the night away. We hadn't been to a club together before, but he knew that it was an activity I had done most weekends with friends to let loose. I appreciated that he now wanted to do it with me. I also knew he loved to see me dressed in form fitting clothing that showed off my figure. When we were out together, his arms protectively resting around my waist, I always felt like his prized possession, like nobody could mess with me, and I liked that.

The night we'd planned to go dancing, he picked me up around 11pm. I wore a white catsuit that hugged all of my curves. Eyeliner, mascara, lip gloss, and heels topped off the look I knew Guy would love. He stood outside his car as I exited the front door, looking at me as if he'd just seen royalty. I indeed felt like his queen. He ran to open the gate for me as I came down the steps. Now face to face, I proceeded to shift some of my hair away from my bare shoulder and allowed him to lay a gentle kiss on it. The kiss sent an enormous sense of calm throughout my entire body.

"What is keeping me from kidnapping you right now to take you somewhere, so I could peel off this number you're wearing to make love to you? Huh?"

I giggled at the thought but insisted, "I've never been dancing with you, so let's stop playing around and go already! After the club, we can conclude the night with you doing all of that, okay?"

"I'm gonna hold you to that!" He opened the door to let me in on the passenger side. After getting in on his side, he caressed my thighs gently before pulling off. The sexual tension was definitely high and I was excited to turn up the heat even higher on the dance floor.

After he found parking, we walked hand in hand to the admission line of the club. As we got closer to it, he seemed on edge, staring at men walking in our direction even though they all passed us. I was hit with a wave of deja vu as I watched his skeptical demeanor, remembering the night we were at the Boston Commons and he became suspicious of the random man who passed us as we sat on the bench. As we walked to the club, he was once again in full paranoid mode. I tried to redirect his attention by kissing him on the cheek and bringing up fun things we had chatted about the night before, but it wasn't working. I no longer felt warm and fuzzy inside. I was now on edge, not sure who or what might set him off. Suddenly it was my sole responsibility to be on my best behavior, so if something did set Guy off, it wouldn't be my fault.

After showing our IDs and paying the cover charge, he led me through the dense crowd until we found a somewhat open spot to settle into. He scanned the crowd around us to make sure there were no threats, and seemed to finally calm down a little as I pulled him face to face with me and started dancing. A popular reggae song I loved had started playing and I was ready for the fun night I had envisioned to begin.

Guy held me around my waist, I threw my arms around his neck, and we danced to the rhythm, completely wrapped up in one another. The DJ was playing all the songs I loved in a row and Guy was feeling them with me. When that set was over, Guy said he wanted to get us drinks, which I was ready for. I had not drunk alcohol in about a year, and reminded him that a Sprite or pineapple juice with no ice would be great. He headed off to the bar, while I remained in our spot and rocked side to side to the DJ's new set. I was enjoying myself. Although Guy had been hyper-vigilant at the beginning of the night, I could tell he was definitely having fun, too.

About two songs played while I waited for Guy to return. Suddenly, another man approached me with a big smile on his face. He began to edge closer to me, looking me up and down a couple times before mouthing something that I couldn't hear over the music. Whatever he was trying to say didn't matter. It only mattered that he was talking to me, so I chose not to respond. I looked the other way in hopes he would get the hint and leave me alone. It didn't work. Soon I felt a warm breath in my ear:

"Damn, you look good, girl..." He was now way too close, so I stepped back to put a little distance between us. As he continued with persistent flirtation, I could only think about Guy coming back from the bar and thinking the worst. This was the exact scenario his paranoia was always guarded against. To try and curtail any of that from happening, I loudly thanked the man for the compliments and asked him to leave before my boyfriend returned from the bar. I told him my boyfriend wouldn't like that he was trying to talk to me, but he refused to budge.

As I continued dismissing the man's advances, I caught sight of Guy out of the corner of my eye. My arms outstretched in the man's direction to keep distance between us, I turned to Guy immediately to explain why this man was in my personal space. Guy, now within ear shot, stood there with our drinks, eyes locked on me instead of the man.

"What's going on here?" Guy asked, still not taking his eyes off me. He had an expression of pure disgust on his face.

"Man, I don't have time for this," he sneered. "I was just trying to pay you a compliment, girl." He stormed off.

"What did you do to invite him over here?" Guy shouted at me over the music. It instantly became clear that he believed my actions had somehow lured the random man into our space. Floored by this thought process, I couldn't think of a response. He put the drinks down on a nearby high top table and approached me to yell, "I can't take you anywhere!"

He grabbed me by my forearm and dragged me quickly through the crowd, toward the exit of the club. Once we exited, he let go of my arm and started walking ahead of me, hurling profanities at the top of his lungs. I was left behind to walk in shame as people passing by looked on in curiosity. I tried to catch up as I followed him in the direction of where the car was parked. At one point, he turned a corner and was out of sight. Speed walking in heels, I hurried to catch up, praying the whole time that he didn't decide to get in his car and leave me downtown alone.

I got closer to the spot where we had parked, and was relieved to see the car was still there. He had already started it and was seated at the wheel. I barely made it into the passenger seat when he hit the gas. The force made the car door slam shut. I buckled up in haste.

Anger was written all over Guy's face as he sped through red lights. I was scared silent, clutching the armrest, wondering if police would spot the car speeding down side streets at 1am and pull us over. He accelerated even more when we got onto the highway, erratically swerving the car from one lane to the other as if he intended to crash into the guardrails.

He kept his left hand on the steering wheel and used his right to grab and choke me. With a firm grip on my throat, he started to yell, "You're a slut! I should have known better, man! That's the kind of dude you want, huh? I couldn't leave you alone for one mother fucking second! You go and humiliate me, letting that fool breathe all over your ass like that. You slut!"

I gasped for air as his grip on my neck became tighter. He let go periodically to regain control of the car, intermittently punching me in the shoulder and upper torso. I was convinced that this was how I was going to die. This was it. Sounds cliche, but my life flashed before my eyes amidst the chaos. Then, almost in an instant, the erratic driving came to an abrupt halt as we exited the highway and came to a stop at the traffic light located at the bottom of the exit ramp.

I was afraid to say anything for fear of riling him up again and triggering another attack. I looked straight ahead, holding my left shoulder and whimpered quietly in pain. I gently touched my neck with my fingertips to see if his nails had broken my skin during the choke holds. It burned to the touch, but there didn't seem to be any blood.

The song *"Summer Rain"* by Carl Thomas played on the car radio. Sometimes Guy would sing the chorus of it to me when it came on. I hoped hearing it now would calm him down some, but Guy stayed silent as we neared my street. As we got closer to my apartment, I wondered how a night so full of promise could go so wrong in what seemed to be an instant. How could he, *again*, think this poorly of me? What could I do to make this right?

He pulled up to the gate, put the car in park, reached over to my door, pushed it open, and shoved me out onto the sidewalk. As I stumbled onto the sidewalk, I heard the car door slam and the tires screech as he sped off into the night. I stood there sobbing as I gathered myself, alone in the dark. I moved quickly because I didn't know if my brothers or Mummy were still up to hear the scramble that had just occurred. They didn't need to know about this. I needed to get it together before I went in. I composed myself the best I could and walked inside.

After tiptoeing to my room and getting undressed, I sat on my bed with my cell phone and called Guy. I needed him to understand that I took full responsibility for what had happened at the club. I wanted to tell him that I should have made an extra effort to get the man away from me. I should have walked away to find Guy at the bar when the man wouldn't leave. It was all my fault, and I needed him to understand that I accepted the blame and that I loved only him. He didn't pick up the first, second, or third time I called; I got his voicemail each time. Finally, he picked up with a one word greeting.

"Yeah?"

Relieved that I finally had the chance to talk to him, I spoke quietly so I wouldn't alert anyone who may be awake that there was anything out of the ordinary happening.

"Baby, I am so, so sorry. You have to know how much I love you! I was worried you would never pick up, but you have to know I can and will do better to show you that you are the only one I want. Please don't throw us away! I love you and only you!"

Guy remained silent as I rambled on.

"I know you do," he finally responded. "I don't want to have to treat you the way I did, but I can't bear the thought of seeing you with someone else. You know you make me do this, right? You make me get this way and I don't want to."

"I know," I whimpered in agreement.

"Do you know where I am right now? At the train station by the train tracks...I'm ready to throw myself onto them when the next train comes because I'm sick at what you made me do. I'm sick about it!"

What was I supposed to do with all that guilt poured onto me at 21 years old? I just accepted it. I did my best to talk him off his suicidal ledge with tons of reassurance, and he in turn promised me that he was not giving up on us and pledged that he would be with me forever.

I had signed up for this. I loved him and was willing to go the distance to prove it. Suffering through a relationship, with little glimmers of hope here and there that things would someday be normal, is what I had learned from watching my parents and my subconscious was a straight-A student in this impossible class.

CHAPTER 8:
Ride or Die

About a year into my relationship with Guy, the Lovern my family and friends knew had all but disappeared. By then, Guy had carelessly thrown around a ton of *forgive me*'s, *I'm sorry*'s, *it won't happen again*'s, and my favorite, *I love you*'s. These words always followed a heightened attack of emotional and verbal abuse or physical beatings to which my body eventually became numb. I mostly just cowered and tried to protect his typical striking spots, but there were a few times I fought back. Guy was bigger and stronger, and when I did try to fight back, he hit me even harder for having the nerve to try. Those few times showed me that I was asking for more trouble, and was not capable of making him stop beating me.

I lived for the high moments where things were calm, but those times seemed to leave as quickly as they came. The love I thought I had for him, my loyalty and concern for his well being, the idea that I needed to see the relationship through to save face, and the hope that it would get better at some point, all factored into why I didn't just pick up and leave.

Mummy and my two younger brothers sometimes overheard me in my room crying or arguing over the phone with him. Whenever they asked if I was okay I got defensive and didn't give much information as to why I was upset, but they knew. Guy had told me over and over that my family didn't understand what we had, that they were jealous of it. He told me no one would ever love me the way he did. Because of the potential conflict between Guy and my family, he was now climbing through my bedroom window to spend the night because my brothers grew to dislike the sight of him. Mummy worked the overnight shift at the hospital, so didn't have to worry about Guy encountering her while sneaking in or out.

One afternoon, the tension came to a head. My brothers and Mummy were scheduled to be out for a while, so Guy came over. Since he was visiting at an unusual time of day, he brought his blood sugar medication with him and placed it in the refrigerator for use later that afternoon. About an hour later when he went to the kitchen to retrieve it, he was surprised to see my youngest brother, Javan, in there too. Guy came back to my room very upset, accusing my brother of tossing his medication in the trash. I was appalled that my brother could have done that, and immediately went out to confront him.

I stepped into the kitchen and sternly asked Javan why he had thrown away Guy's medication. He vehemently denied the accusation.

"I didn't do anything! If that punk ass thinks I did, he can come accuse me to my face!" Javan yelled at the top of his lungs. "He should get out of our house! He doesn't belong here!"

At this point Guy had come out of the bedroom to respond to my brother's hysterics with a smirk, calmly stating, "You know what you did." He gathered his keys, walked past my brother, and exited the house through the front door. Javan followed him to continue the argument. I followed them both in haste.

On the sidewalk, Javan's voice became much louder. The fight escalated fast, and I was resolute in siding with Guy. Javan pulled out a knife, threatening to use it on Guy if he didn't get in his car and leave. That's when I decided to call the police in hopes they would help to diffuse the situation. Amidst all of this, Sean came home and immediately sided with Javan, yelling for Guy and me to leave, adding that I should stay gone and never come back because I was a traitor for siding with the enemy. I hung up my cell phone and I asked Guy to get in the car and wait for me, afraid that Javan would charge at him with the knife at any moment. I quickly ran inside, grabbed my jacket, ran back to his car, and got inside with him. With both my brothers still yelling, we sat there and waited for the cops to arrive.

It didn't take long before a police cruiser pulled up. After the officers assessed the situation, talking to both sides, they placed handcuffs on Javan for attempting to use a weapon. I never expected that this was going to be the outcome. As they loaded him into their car, Sean continued to hurl words of contempt at us. The police advised Guy that he should leave the premises, so I left with him. Driving away from the house, I felt sick to my stomach about the whole situation. After much convincing later that evening, he agreed to take me to the police station to drop all the charges.

We walked into the station's lobby to find Mummy, Sean, and some extended family members all looking at Guy and me as if we were the scum of the earth. Their stares cut deep into my core and made me feel ashamed and responsible for everything that had happened since I was the one who called the police. I walked up to the window and asked the officer if I could bail my brother out and drop any charge against him.

"I'm sorry, ma'am. You'll have to wait until Monday. He'll go before a judge, and the judge will determine what happens."

A weekend in jail? He would have to be there all weekend? This news made me even more sick. Stepping away from the window, I assumed that my family had already received this information. It now made sense that they were disgusted with the sight of us. Realizing that nothing could be done, I left the station in disbelief that this was really happening. I could not go back home now. I was a traitor and Guy was the only person left on my side.

He drove to a street unfamiliar to me, which I expected since anywhere personal to him was unfamiliar. When we pulled up, he said he was going to briefly see a friend of his. *No problem*, I thought, *we'll probably head to his place afterward*. He parked the car more than a few houses away from his final destination and walked the rest, leaving me in the car. I was too despondent from all that had transpired earlier that day to try and figure out why he hadn't parked in front of the house he was going to. He returned about half an hour later.

"We're gonna have to sleep in the car tonight, but everything's gonna be okay," Guy blurted out after closing the car door and starting the car. I was stunned! Did he just say we were going to have to sleep in his car? Where was his apartment?

Something like this shouldn't have been okay with me, but it became okay in that moment. I was on the outs with my family and going home was not an option. Friends were slim to none after a year of blowing them off. I would need a few more weeks of pay before I had enough in my savings to find an apartment of my own, so this was it. The whole scenario was starting to feel like a real Bonnie and Clyde deal. Me and Guy against the world.

We went to a drive-through for dinner, then drove to the park close to my job. He parked in a lot that was attached to a baseball field, the spot where we would settle for the night, and ate. After dinner, we talked about how we would get out of the situation. "We" actually meant me since he was still laid off from work and wouldn't be able to help me afford an apartment.

It began to get dark and the amount of people in the park lessened. My initial plan was to keep my eyes open all night because I was scared, but the weight of the day was wearing on me. When I told Guy how exhausted I was, he draped his coat over me for warmth and volunteered to stay awake to make sure nobody approached the car as I slept. As my eyelids got heavier, it sunk in that I was now a homeless professional, sleeping in a car with the person who often harmed me and was now serving as my protector. I reclined the passenger seat all the way back and closed my eyes with that fact heavy on my mind.

I woke up several times during the night and checked to make sure Guy was still there. He always was. After an uncomfortable sleep, I awoke the next morning to see him already wide awake at the wheel. Once he saw I was up, he suggested we drive to the nearby fast food restaurant to use the bathroom and wash up. I used the toilet, then waited for the last person to exit before hurriedly using the sink to brush my teeth and wash up. Back at the car, Guy and I used the drive-through to get breakfast and then drove to the nearby mall and waited for it to open. I bought some clothes and other necessities for the week and stored everything in the trunk of the car.

We passed the time that day watching movies at the mall's movie theater. Guy slept through most of them after staying up the entire night before. After the movies we headed back to the park for a few hours, grabbed dinner, and ended the day back at the spot where we had camped out the night before. We repeated the already-familiar routine of Guy staying up all night to keep watch. He was in full protective mode.

The next morning he dropped me off at work. With no access to a steamer or iron, I had purchased wrinkle free items from the mall. I walked into the office that morning looking happy-go-lucky on the outside, but feeling like scum and filth on the inside. I had become pretty good at masking the chaos that lay within. Nobody suspected how my life had shifted over the weekend.

At lunch, I stepped outside to call the police station and find out my brother's status. They told me I needed to call the courthouse for details of his bail, so I did that and I found out Javan had been released on his own recognizance. I was relieved, but knew I was still a sister scorned and could not return home. Some of what Guy had spent months drumming into my psyche rang especially true in that moment: Guy was the only one who loved me, because no one else understood us or our love.

The physical abuse mostly dwindled during the time we spent living in his car. Many of the attributes that made me fall in love with him were back. Even though we were homeless, I settled back into the comfort of our relationship.

***

For the next two weeks, I took showers at the beach's rinse shower stalls in South Boston and slept in that parking lot. I was actively looking for an affordable one-bedroom apartment, but everything was too far out of my price range until I came across a listing for a studio space about ten minutes away from where I had lived with Mummy and my brothers. Guy and I set up an appointment to go look at it.

On the day of the showing, we pulled up to a tall, vine-covered brown-stone that was quaint but charming. The first thing I loved about the apartment was the location, directly next to major bus and train lines that would make it incredibly convenient to get to work. The neighborhood was also in good condition, with a collection of eateries and convenience stores nearby and scenic side streets for running or taking long walks.

We headed up to the apartment on the third floor, which looked out at the building's courtyard. The door opened up to the bedroom, a very long space that connected to the kitchen on one end and the bathroom on the other. Though the apartment was on the smaller side, it was priced right, clean, and modern looking. After filling out the rental application, I waited on pins and needles for a few more days until I got a call back saying the space was mine. I was ecstatic to have a roof over my head again.

At the Peabody Apartment Building's Courtyard

After signing on the dotted line, I was excited to set up my new space. I bought a daybed that served as a sofa during the day, and Guy accompanied me to a nearby rent-to-own furniture store where I picked out a dresser. He also insisted on a wide-screen TV and DVD-VCR combo so he could watch sports and movies when he was over, so I added those to the list. All the furniture was delivered and set up on my move-in day. After the basics were in the apartment Guy and I went shopping for cleaning, bedroom, and kitchen essentials. The entire process felt so grown-up, but nothing made me happier than no longer living out of a vehicle.

About a week after moving in, I was settled. Guy and I were making good use of the space by taking candle-lit bubble baths together, dancing cheek to cheek in the bedroom to our favorite songs, and rustling up dinner as a pair in the kitchen. He even started watching crime dramas and Lifetime Movies with me. We had been through a rough patch in the first year of dating, but now I believed he saw how loyal and focused on the relationship I was. I thought things were great.

The second week in the apartment, Guy stood at the kitchen counter making us sandwiches when he asked about the man who lived a couple doors down.

"Huh?" I responded, perplexed.

He wanted to know if I had ever seen him around, and what I thought of him. I told him I didn't have any thoughts about him, since I barely noticed the man until Guy brought him up. It seemed like my answer had appeased him since the rest of the afternoon passed without incident, but I had an awful feeling in the pit of my stomach that this honeymoon phase we'd been living in would be over soon.

Guy became increasingly jealous of the man down the hall over the next few months. He appeared to be a young professional who lived alone, sometimes bringing home female guests. He was cordial whenever he saw us but otherwise never had any interaction with me. Even though the man never did anything but mind his own business, Guy always managed to make him a topic of conversation.

"Were you talking to him today?"

"Did he pop over here earlier to talk to you or something?"

"I see the way he looks at you when we walk by. You know he's gonna try something sooner or later, right?"

"That's the kinda guy you want, right? A player with a fancy job and shit, right? I know you've been checking him out. If I went into his crib, would I find your panties there? Huh?"

I had finally received peace and normalcy for a brief moment after moving into the apartment, and now they were gone again because of this imaginary attraction Guy had conjured between me and the man down the hall. Each accusation was more extreme than the last, which led me to believe that Guy was coming up with reasons to beat me. Once again, my gut instinct was right.

Guy walked into the apartment one afternoon after a job interview he felt had gone badly. I went to greet him with a kiss, but he pushed me away.

"There's no way I got that fucking job, which is bullshit. I mean, why'd they even call me in for an interview! Meanwhile, pussies like homeboy down the hall get hired everyday! Dudes like that aren't even as qualified as me, but that's the kinda dude you probably wanna be with, right?" He asked angrily from the kitchen as I sat on the bed, startled from his severe attitude.

"You want him every time you see him, right? Did he flirt with you today? I bet you would like that shit, huh? You probably wanna move in and be with him 'cause you think I'm a loser!"

I listened to him in bewilderment. Now in the bedroom space, standing over me, Guy grabbed and squeezed me by my forearms. He shoved me onto the daybed and started punching me all over my body while I was down.

Crunched into the fetal position and trying to simultaneously protect my sides and face, I processed the familiar, evil look on his face and the devilish tone in his voice. The blows hurt, but the pain concerned me less than crying quietly enough that neighbors wouldn't hear me. *I could easily explain his loud voice if someone questioned me,* I thought. *I could say that he was upset about the way his sports team was playing. Just protect my sides and breasts. Protect my face. Curl up. Get smaller. It will be over soon. Just be quiet.*

When the attack was finally over Guy stormed out of the apartment without a word, slamming the door behind him. I struggled to get myself up, finding I was able to waddle over and lock the door. Before I did, I opened it and took a peek into the hallway to make sure no one overheard the attack. Relief washed over me when I saw there was no one there. I took myself to bed, curled up to ease the pain, and cried myself to sleep.

CHAPTER 9:
Wearing A Mask

After I had been in the apartment for a couple months I reconnected with a high school friend, Amanda, when she moved into a house directly behind my apartment building. We didn't see each other a lot, but we exchanged phone numbers and would chat sometimes when Guy was not around. It felt good to have a friend nearby. Guy didn't seem threatened by her if he saw me talking to her in person, and Amanda never questioned me if I had to hang up suddenly. It always felt like she knew more than she let on about what was happening to me behind closed doors, but she didn't judge me.

There were no more elaborate dates for Guy and I. Instead, he set a routine for me that was pretty much set in stone: work during the day, school at night, grocery shopping, and trips to the rent-to-own furniture company to make my weekly payments. Guy always accompanied me when running this particular errand, because the store was full of male sales representatives that he didn't trust around me. In the beginning he made a point to hug on me tightly as I completed the payment transaction. He relaxed as time went on, eventually allowing me to go in by myself with a seven minute window to get back to the car. The salesmen, causally funny men who seemed to always be joking around, had caught on to Guy's jealous nature and would joke with me about it when I came in alone.

"How come your man isn't plastered on your back today?" one of the more boisterous salesmen asked. This made the other employees all chuckle.

"Look, I give him two more minutes before he comes in here to claim his dime piece, because he never lets her out of his sight!" he continued, prompting even more laughter from the group.

"You are all crazy..." I replied good-naturedly.

But they weren't crazy; they had honed in on Guy's obvious paranoia. I needed them to see the Lovern who had it together. It was all part of the charade I lived daily. As long as I kept my mask of a capable professional woman tightly secured, no one would know that my boyfriend beat me and I was a weak, helpless girl.

I knew their playing around was eating up precious minutes and if I went over my allotted time, Guy would get suspicious. I tried to get them to speed up my payment. "Could you finish up, 'cause I have to..."

My sentence was interrupted by all the salesmen erupting in laughter as they looked past me toward the entrance of the store. Guy was now inside looking for me, just as the salesmen had predicted. It took everything in me to not laugh with them, but needed to get my face together so he would not figure out that the joke was about him.

When Guy reached me at the counter, he asked the group what was so funny. Before I could answer, the salesmen covered it up by saying they were just talking about a customer who had tripped and fallen earlier that day. The one taking my payment added his own apology, taking the blame for the transaction being extra long since their system was running slow that day. Guy seemed to accept that explanation. The group of salesmen disbanded, and one helping me finished up, keeping everything completely professional. When it was done I was relieved to head back to the car. Guy held my hand as we walked out of the store.

"What took you so long?" He asked after getting settled in the driver's seat.

"Well, there were just a few customers ahead of me when I walked in, and like he said, their stupid system was really slow today for some reason." Guy believed me, and I continued to be allowed to enter the store solo to make my monthly payments while he waited in the car. During future visits, the salesmen always made light of Guy's obsessive personality, but also hurried my transaction along so he wouldn't need to come in and fetch me again.

Living with an abusive partner can make it especially hard to identify or create opportunities to leave. Here are some steps an advocate can help you take to help prepare to leave an abusive living situation, keeping in mind that everyone's situation will look different:

- *Identify safe areas in your residence with pathways to exit, away from any weapons. If arguments occur, try to move to those areas before they escalate.*
- *If safe, have a phone accessible at all times to call 911 for help, including friends or family, and your local shelter.*
- *Know where the nearest public phone is located.*

- *Let trusted friends and neighbors know about your situation and develop a plan and visual or verbal signal for help. Give them clear instructions on who you want them to contact in moments of crisis.*
- *Talk to others living in the residence how to get help, including children or roommates. Instruct them not to get physically involved in violence between you and your partner and work with them to establish a signal for when they should call to get help or leave the house to get help.*
- *Create several plausible reasons for leaving the house at different times of the day or night: multiple trips to the grocery store, spending time with friends, staying at work longer or finding unnecessary errands to complete.*
- *If possible, practice how to get out safely, including with children who may be living in the home.*
- *If possible, keep weapons like guns and knives locked away and stored as inaccessibly as possible.*
- *Back your car into your driveway when you park at home and keep it fueled. If possible, keep a spare set of keys hidden in the car with the driver's door unlocked and the rest of the doors locked to allow for quick access to the vehicle.*
- *If violence is unavoidable, make yourself as physically small as possible. Move to a corner and curl into a ball with your face protected and arms around each side of your head, fingers entwined.*

CHAPTER 10:
The Breaking Point

I lived inside the charade of a healthy relationship, and I was getting exhausted from constantly keeping up the show. I couldn't look left or right as we sat in traffic because Guy considered that an invitation for attention from men in other cars. I couldn't stand in close proximity to the security guard while waiting for Guy to pick me up because he believed the guards tried to flirt with me. I couldn't miss his calls during the work day, because he assumed that meant I was flirting with male colleagues or talking on the phone to male friends. I didn't know how much longer I could go on like this, hoping and wishing for a future with him that didn't involve drama.

One Friday night around 9:00, Guy stormed into the apartment pissed at the world. He hurled his typical accusations that I had had someone over earlier in the day while he wasn't there. I assured him I hadn't. He accused me of talking to my neighbor on the phone. I assured him I didn't. He grabbed my cell phone and started going through my call history, but found nothing and tossed it back at me.

He began rummaging through my belongings, vigorously shaking each book in a stack of novels on top of my dresser. I was an avid reader and had read most of those books multiple times after moving to the States. I sat on the daybed and watched as he conducted his paranoid search. *Here we go again,* I thought. *He's looking for an excuse to unleash on me.*

Guy picked up a book my aunt had given me, *Waiting to Exhale* by Terry McMillan. It was one of my favorites and the basis for the movie that famously starred Whitney Houston. He held the book by it's spine and shook it, just as he had done with the others. To my surprise, a picture fell out onto the floor. I wondered which one it was as he bent over to pick it up. He stood up and stared intently at the photo, his face turning the reddest I had ever seen it. My heart raced as I wondered what could have made him so angry. He flung the picture at me and stormed into the kitchen where it sounded like he was banging utensils together.

Dread flooded my system when I looked at the picture. I knew exactly the story Guy was making up in his head as he clattered around my kitchen. It was a photo of me with my Trinidadian ex-boyfriend, whom I had dated briefly before coming back to the States the second time. It showed my then-boyfriend and I sitting at the beach, hugged up tight and looking happy. He had suggested we do the long distance thing, but that lasted all of two weeks before I found out that he was dating another girl on the island, so I moved on with my life in the States. Prior to our breakup, I had used this picture of us as a bookmark for *Waiting to Exhale*. It had been in the book so long that I'd forgotten all about it. Petrified, I tried to explain this to Guy from the daybed. When he re-entered the bedroom, Guy was holding a long knife from the kitchen. A knife! This was the first time he had ever drawn a weapon near me.

"So, you've been making a fool out of me this entire time? I knew you were too be good to be true, you fucking slut! You been having phone sex with him? Huh? Wiring money to him?" He primed the knife in one hand and balled his fist with the other. "I'm gonna kill you tonight for making a fool outta me, and no one's gonna find you!"

I believed him. Who would come looking for me if he decided to stab me and leave me there, or get rid of my body? Not my family. I hadn't spoken to them in months. Not my friends. I was hardly in contact with any of them at this point. Not my neighbors. They would probably continue to mind their own business. Not my job. They probably wouldn't even notice my absence was permanent for at least a few days.

Guy pushed me down on the daybed and towered over me, kneeling on my palms. He used one hand to squeeze my throat and the other to press the knife against my neck. He pressed hard enough to let me know that he could slit my throat at any time if I tried to resist him. There was nothing on his face except blind rage and fury. He looked like a rabid dog foaming at the mouth.

After far too long, he put the knife to the side. He spat in my face, screamed and yelled, and slapped me repeatedly. This wasn't one of his regular attacks; he hadn't slapped me since that very first incident at my grandparent's house, because I worked in a corporate setting where he knew people would ask questions about any bruises on my face. Tonight, that logic was apparently not enough to deter a facial attack.

He put his hand around my neck and choked me again. I must have passed out at some point, because when I came to, he was no longer on top of me. He paced the floor back and forth with the knife in his hand, muttering to himself: "I can't believe I tried to make a slut into a housewife. How dare you fuck with me and try to make a fucking fool outta me!" When he realized I was conscious, Guy straddled me on the bed again and repeated the attack. He pressed the knife against my throat as he cursed me, then put it down to punch me in the torso and hips. It seemed he would only stop to pace the floor and take breathing breaks before starting the terrifying cycle over again.

He repeated this process until about 2:00 the next morning: stop and pace about, then back to punching, choking, spitting, knife wielding, and making sure I felt the sharp blade's pressure on my skin. Then, suddenly, he just stopped. He dropped the knife to the floor, got into bed next to me, and cursed at me until he fell asleep. I lay there whimpering, paralyzed with the fear of waking the beast. If I chose to run, I didn't know who I could call or where I could go.

At 4:00 I was still laying in bed contemplating how I could possibly have let things get this bad, when I began to feel sharp pains in my midsection. My body had become numb to the blows from prior attacks, but the pain from this one felt like daggers trying to pierce through my skin. I was no medical professional, but had seen enough crime TV where people died from internal bleeding or untreated broken bones. The severity of the pain told me something was seriously wrong. I had a choice to make: stay there and let Guy increase the intensity of the next attack that might leave me dead, or survive and get help. I decided to survive.

I got up and dressed very quietly, grabbed my jacket, wallet and keys, walked out the door, and hobbled down the stairs. I exited the apartment building, rounded the corner, and got into the first cab I saw. One of the advantages of living next door to a train station was that you never lacked transportation. The nearest hospital was only about ten blocks away, and the black male driver agreed to take me there. I winced in pain as I climbed into the backseat. He noticed me struggling to sit down.

"You okay, Miss?" he asked with a French-sounding accent.

I was not okay. I was scared out of my mind. "I'm fine," I hurriedly told the driver, so he would get me as far away from my building as possible.

There were only two traffic lights between my building and the hospital, and the first one we met was red. We sat in silence, waiting for it to turn green. This intersection was usually busy, but at the early hour of the morning there was only us and one other car next to us. The car next to us was pumping loud music, and it only took me a few seconds to realize it was Guy! He must have realized I left and seen me get into the cab. As I stared at him in terror, Guy turned his radio down and began yelling at me, "Get out of the fuckin' cab!"

I instinctively locked the cab's back doors and turned to the driver, who was alarmed by all the commotion Guy was making. I quickly rummaged through my wallet and handed him a $10 bill, which would more than cover the fare.

"You need change?" he asked.

"No I don't, but I am begging you, please do not let me out of this cab! If you do, I am as good as dead! That is my *ex*-boyfriend and he is going to kill me if you let me out! Run the light if you have to so he doesn't get to me! I am begging you!" It was the first time I had referred to Guy as my ex, and the first time I'd voiced to anyone just how scared I was that he could do real damage to me.

The driver looked at me, his eyes wide with confusion, then shifted his gaze to Guy, who was still yelling and gesturing frantically. The driver quickly turned forward and accelerated, running the light just as I had begged him to. I looked out the rear window to see Guy speeding through the light as well, quickly catching up in the lane next to us. With only a short distance left to get to the hospital, Guy revved his engine and kept pace with the cab until the cab took a quick turn into the hospital's main entrance. I looked back to see that Guy's car had come to a full stop in the middle of the street instead of following us into the lot. I watched as he sped away, giving up the horrifying chase.

When the cab driver finally pulled up in front of the emergency room doors, he put the car in park and turned around to look at me. His face was a mix of worry and care. "I will be praying for you, my sista. That man seemed determined. I pray you will be safe!"

With that, he unlocked all the doors for me to get out. I thanked him repeatedly as I stepped away from the vehicle that had just gotten me out of my very own Lifetime Movie scene.

Some reasons why victims choose not to report domestic violence:

- *Their abuser prevented them using physical force.*
- *Their abuser pleaded with them not to report.*
- *Family members/friends prevented them from reporting.*
- *They were embarrassed/ashamed.*
- *They believed it was a private and personal matter.*
- *The incident seemed too trivial/unimportant.*
- *They believed there was nothing police could do.*
- *Bad/disappointing experience with reporting previous incidents to police.*
- *Did not want the abuser to get in trouble.*

Source: *Page 5, https://www.women.nsw.gov.au/__data/assets/ pdf_file/0004/280912/Reporting_Violence_to_the_Police_-_BOCSAR_ survey.pdf*

CHAPTER 11:
What Help Means

Taking myself to the emergency room was a new and daunting task. I initially walked in with a sigh of relief, followed by a load of crippling shame. I was relieved that Guy had stopped following me, but ashamed of how the nurses might look at me once I told them what brought me there. I also still loved Guy and didn't want him to get in trouble. I just wanted the abuse to stop.

I took a seat in the waiting area and thought through all sorts of scenarios I could describe to the intake person. I needed a story that would show them I was in a lot of pain, but wouldn't bring unnecessary attention to my situation. As the possibilities swirled around inside my head, the triage nurse called my name and asked the dreaded question: "What brings you here today?"

"I slipped and fell in the shower. I ended up hitting my upper torso and hip areas. Think something might be broken. I dunno."

"Which side of your torso and hip?" she asked.

"It was a bit of a tumble and I hit both sides. They both hurt really bad."

I hoped she believed me. She finished up the intake and asked me to have a seat once again. After another short wait, I was sent to get X-rays. Things were moving faster than I had thought they would, but that made sense since it was so early in the morning and I was one of the only people waiting to be helped.

It was cold in the X-ray room, but the tech was personable and made the process as quick as possible. After that, another nurse walked me to an exam area with a bed, where the only borders between my area and the next patient's were thin fabric curtains. Not private at all, but I got undressed and put on the unflattering hospital gown she provided. Whoever designed these things had not considered cases like mine; I was in too much pain to reach around my back to tie the strings and had to ask the nurse for help.

After getting dressed, I sat at the edge of the bed and waited for the doctor to come in and give me his prognosis. As I waited, I thought about whether or not I was doing the right thing by even being there. Now that I was seeking help, would Guy retaliate?

Where in the world is this doctor? I thought. It felt close to an hour that I had been left alone with my thoughts when I heard a voice on the other side of the curtain.

"Ms. Anderson? Is it okay to come in?"

"Um, yeah, it's okay," I responded hastily.

The doctor entered and shook my hand, introducing himself as Dr. Stewart. He sat on a small black rolling chair and opened the manilla folder in his hand.

"I was waiting for your X-rays to come back," he said, explaining why I had to wait for so long in the curtained room. "So, what's going on?" he asked with a quizzical expression on his face.

I was annoyed by his question because although his words came off as understanding, I felt like he should already know what the deal was. "Isn't that info in your file there? I told the nurses what happened already," I snapped.

"I know you did, but these injuries aren't consistent with you falling down in the shower. Who did this to you?" His eyes now felt judgemental.

What? How in the world could he have known it was a "who" and not a "what" that caused this? Was he trying to trip me up and catch me in a lie? Did the nurses see through my lies and give him a heads up? Did the cab driver call the cops after he drove off, and now there were police right outside the room waiting to question me?

I clammed up. The room was silent as we both waited for the other to speak.

"If you tell me the truth, I can get you help," Dr. Stewart added.

Help? What does that even mean? I rubbed my sweaty palms together, trying to process the concept of help. To me, it translated to the police showing up at my apartment building. My neighbors seeing me as nothing but the black woman bringing drama to their building. My family finally finding out the extent of Guy's abuse and blaming me for it. I could hear it now from my extended family members: "How could you *let yourself* go through this, knowing what your mother went through?" I could hear both of my brother's voices in my head: "How could you *let* that clown treat you like that? You're stupid for *letting* him do that to you, and for siding with him against us!"

"Help" meant my teachers at school finding out why I was on track to flunking my freshman year of college. I was never able to focus during class, and I got lousy grades on any group assignments that involved male classmates. Guy ruined every study group by calling my cell phone repeatedly, forcing me to tell him the address of the meeting, and showing up if he thought I was taking too long. It was embarrassing and scary.

Letting this doctor "help" me meant my boss and colleagues finding out why I sometimes came back to my desk looking upset. Guy sometimes showed up at my job under the guise of wanting to take me to lunch, but then accosted me in the lobby if he thought the skirt I was wearing that day was too short and inviting the attention of the men in the office. After a verbal tirade or a substantial chokehold to let me know just how upset he was, he would storm off and leave me in the lobby. After a trip to the bathroom to wash my face, I would return to my desk and do my best to look like nothing had happened. I was one of only two women of color at the office, and feared being labeled with a stereotype if my colleagues found out what sometimes happened at lunch. I worked hard not to be labeled as the black girl whose personal affairs were disruptive to the work environment, and "help" would potentially ruin that.

Leaning on my wide knowledge of TV shows, I thought the doctor would probably suggest that I go to a shelter. I envisioned a shelter as a big open room with beds full of women I didn't know, and I wasn't interested in that. I only wanted to go home and lock the world out, so in response to the doctor's offer of help, I remained silent.

"Look," Dr. Stewart said, "You don't have to be afraid. If you don't want to give details, I understand. If you decide to open up, here's my card, okay?" He fished a business card out of his white coat pocket and held it out. I took it and slid it under my leg on the bed.

I sighed to myself. Who was I fooling? He could see through the lies because he held the black and white truth in that manilla folder. He had also probably seen this type of case multiple times before from other women.

"Okay, listen. My *ex*-boyfriend got a little aggressive with me after he thought I had done something bad, but I didn't. I don't want any police involved. What we say here is confidential, right?" I had now referred to Guy as my ex, part of my past, to two different people in one day.

"Yes, it most certainly is. If you don't want me to press, I understand. Are you going to be okay? Will you be safe at home? I can give you information for other help once you leave here." The look on his face had now changed from judgemental to concerned.

"I'll be fine. I just want to go home."

Help was daunting and scary and I wanted no part of it.

"Well, the good news is nothing is broken. You have what are called contusions on your upper torso and hip areas, where you complained of pain." He reached into the manilla folder and pulled out one of the X-rays as he spoke. He pointed to an area on it as he explained that blunt force from the impact of the blows Guy had delivered over the course of the five-hour attack had caused my flesh to become swollen and bruised on the inside. Thankfully, these contusions could be treated with pain medication, icing the affected areas, and lots of rest. As I watched Dr. Stewart write up instructions for the nurse, I thought of my mother and how many untreated contusions she had suffered over the years. I was now resolute that I couldn't return to Guy ever again if I didn't want to end up back at the hospital.

Dr. Stewart asked me once again if I would be okay to return home by myself. I assured him I would be.

CHAPTER 12:
Disclosure

I picked up my prescription from a nearby pharmacy and went home. Upon entering my apartment, I used all my might to push my tall dresser in front of the door to block it. If Guy tried to come back to finish me off, he wouldn't be able to get in easily. This makeshift barricade would give me time to call for help. I was scared to death.

He's probably really mad thinking I outed him. He probably really thinks I messed up. Even after everything that happened, his feelings were still the first thing on my mind.

I unplugged my landline phone, turned off my cell, and kept all the lights off. I cocooned myself in blankets on the daybed where the attack had taken place and held ice packs on my hips and belly until I cried myself to sleep. The meds made me drowsy and I slept through the night until Sunday morning. When I awoke, I emailed my boss to tell her I wouldn't be in on Monday because of a stomach bug. This gave me one more day to rest and hopefully not look like a truck had run over me.

I decided I needed to build up enough courage to tell someone at the leasing office that I wanted my building's locks changed. I couldn't keep pushing the dresser in front of the door each time I came home. It was heavy, and moving it aggravated my injuries. I would have to suck the shame up and tell someone what had happened so they could secure the entrance to my building.

That Monday morning, still a little groggy from the pain meds, I got dressed and slowly made my way down to the leasing office. When I opened my apartment door, I peeped down the hallway to make sure it was empty. When I got to the end of the hallway, I leaned over the banister to check as far down as I could to see whether the coast was clear. When I got to the bottom of the stairs, I peered out from the mailbox before heading outside in the direction of the office. I had to make sure Guy wasn't lurking somewhere, waiting to hurt me. I was now one of those women who was always looking over her shoulder.

I entered the office and was met by a familiar representative to whom I usually turned in my monthly rent payments.

"Hi Lovern, how are you?" she asked when I walked in. I had always liked this rep. She was always cheerful and welcoming, and we had great rapport. She reminded me of Topanga from the *Boy Meets World* sitcom. "Are you okay?" she asked with concern when she saw me writing in pain as I tried to take a seat in the chair.

"I'm okay, but I need some help." I struggled to get comfortable to no avail, so I stood up slowly and decided to finish the exchange standing. "I'm not sure where to start and it's really embarrassing. I broke up with my boyfriend over the weekend but I don't feel safe. I am afraid he's going to come by and be very upset when I tell him to his face that I'm through. He has a key to the building and my door, and I'm wondering how to go about getting the locks to both of them changed?"

As I spoke, Topanga's demeanor changed from caring to apprehensive. Her face flushed as she searched for an answer to my question. "Ummm, oh my goodness! Well… ummm, I'm not sure… I'll have to reach out to my manager and get back to you."

As I watched her stumble through the explanation, all I could think was, *Calgon, take me away!* I felt she would no longer see me as a professional woman. She would definitely gossip with her coworkers that I got beat up. I would probably even be asked to vacate the apartment because I posed a safety risk. I didn't know what else to do to keep myself safe besides speaking up and asking for this lock change, but in that moment, I felt like it was the wrong thing to do.

Topanga and I usually exchanged cheerful small talk about the weather or work, and she sometimes commented admiringly on my fashion sense. There was none of that today. We both wanted the exchange to be over, and it showed.

"Okay, thanks. I'll wait for you guy's call on what's next," I said.

"Uh, yep… I'm putting a note in your file since they aren't around today."

"Okay great, thanks." I turned to the door and headed out as fast as I could, which wasn't fast enough for me.

I got a call from the office manager within the hour. Topanga had said that whoever dealt with lock changes wasn't around, so that must have meant my drama was a priority that needed to be handled ASAP!

"Hi, Ms. Anderson. This is Erica from the Leasing Office for The Peabody Building." Her voice was cold and businesslike. I didn't recognize her name, and she didn't sound like someone I wanted to get to know.

"Hi there," I responded.

"I understand you have some safety concerns and want the locks to your apartment and main door changed?" She sounded like an aristocrat getting ready to scold somebody who was beneath her.

"Yes, that's correct."

"Have you reported your concerns to the police?"

"No, but I plan to later today." I wasn't going to the police, but knew I needed to say this to appease her.

"Well, we can have someone come by tomorrow morning, but you will have to pay for it since you are putting other residents' safety in jeopardy."

What? I was being treated like a liability. "Uhhhh... okay... um... I understand."

"Someone from the office will let you know later today what time the locksmith will be by. You don't need to be home. Please stop by the office for the invoice and new set of keys. We'll add the amount of the charge to your next month's rent."

"Ok. Will do. Thank you."

I hung up feeling like a complete disgrace. This was the first time I had spoken up voluntarily, and it made me feel like a nuisance. I wondered if protecting myself from Guy was worth the shame I felt every time I disclosed even a small detail of what he had done to me.

Leaving is not easy. On average, it takes a victim seven times to leave before staying away for good. Exiting the relationship is the most unsafe time for a victim. As the abuser senses that they're losing power, they will often act in dangerous or manipulative ways to regain control over their victim.

Source: *https://www.thehotline.org/resources/50-obstacles-to-leaving/*

CHAPTER 13:
Life or Loyalty

Two weeks passed and Guy didn't call or show up. I went through a range of emotions after the attack: self-pity, self-doubt, shame, anger, sadness, fear. Many times, I thought about picking up the phone to let him know that even though I still loved him, I had to leave because I believed our dynamic would only get worse. Sometimes I even thought of returning to him. I wanted him to comfort me the way he did after an attack, to tell me how much he loved me and that he would do better for real going forward so we didn't have to break up. He would realize he had taken things way too far, and he would get help to stop being that way. It felt almost like I was detoxing from an addiction to Guy. It took a lot of restraint not to dial his number.

One afternoon after taking a shower, I sat on the floor of my bedroom putting rollers in my wet hair and watching the Lifetime Movie channel on TV. Suddenly, my landline phone rang. It was connected to a live answering machine so I could screen my calls. My hands were occupied, so I let the call go to voicemail.

"Baby. Lovern. Pick up." It was Guy! His voice sent chills down my spine. I moved closer to the answering machine where his voice had paused, waiting on the other end of the line for me to pick up. My stomach in knots, I waited for his next set of words. Click! He hung up. Within seconds the phone rang again. I let it go to voicemail again as I searched my frenzied mind for what to do.

Looking back, I know he felt comfortable enough to call me that day because he had waited two weeks to see if any heat would come his way. Heat, as in trouble for him, after the attack that landed me in the ER. My brothers hadn't confronted him during that time. The police hadn't shown up to ask him any questions. He now knew that I had kept silent about the assault and thought it was safe to pick up where he had left off.

"Listen, pick up the phone." His tone was serious and a little demanding, which scared me even more. "I know you're there. Right about now you must be taking in a little Lifetime and doing your hair, so what's the problem? Why aren't you picking up the damn phone? Pick up the damn phone!" He started to breathe heavily as the demands got louder.

Click! He hung up again but the phone immediately rang once more. I continued to stare at it instead of picking it up. Although I was afraid of just the sound of his voice, I also felt a little power in not having to rush to answer his every attempt to contact me.

The answering machine beeped as he began yet another message.

"Listen, you fucking bitch! I dunno who the fuck you got over there that's keeping you from answering my calls, but you better understand, you are *mine*! You hear me? You are *mine* and you need to stop fucking around and answer the motherfucking phone!"

After another four back-to-back phone calls, I was ready to tell him I was done. The next time it rang, I picked up before it could go to voicemail and said nothing.

"Hello?" he said to my silence.

"What do you want, Guy?"

"What do I want? Don't get fucking flip with me. Who do you think you are, and who the fuck you got over there? Didn't you hear me calling all those times before? You think I got all day to be playing with you?" I rolled my eyes as he continued. "I'm about to come over there, cause we gotta talk!"

It made me angry that he thought he could just come over to talk, as if it was business as usual. Up to this point he mentioned nothing about the assault, so I did. "Under no circumstances are you allowed to come here. I had the locks changed. Do I need to remind you that you almost killed me two weeks ago? Did you forget how you punched the hell out of me and then fell asleep as if nothing happened when you were through?"

When he replied, his voice was dripping with snark. "Mannnnn, you know you looked for that. Enough with all this. I'll be over there in a few. Forget this dumb shit about changing locks. You better have a new key waiting for me if you really decided to do some dumb ass shit like that!" *Click!* He was done with the tirade and off the phone. This exchange reminded me why I had chosen to be done with him in the first place. It also reminded me of my father's response when he blamed Mummy for his attacks on her. I was repulsed by it all.

I didn't believe his threat about coming over. He would have no way of getting in and it would be embarrassing for people to see him trying to do so. I knew from previous experience that Guy wasn't too keen on public shame. *Good riddance,* I thought, feeling safe in my resolve. I resumed adding the last few rollers to my now semi-dry hair.

About fifteen minutes later, there was a knock at my door. "Lovern, it's me. Open up. I need to talk to you."

How in the freaking world did he get into the building? I thought. He must have waited until someone exited the main door and slipped inside. However he'd managed it, he was here now, and there was only a slab of wood between us. All the courage I had summoned when he was only a voice on the other end of the phone vanished. I was paralyzed with fear. I wasn't sure if the door was secure enough to keep him out, and had no idea how I would protect myself if it wasn't.

"Guy, listen. Please listen to me! I know you don't wanna talk. You have to leave right now! I'm not opening the door, so please, please leave!"

"Open the fucking door, Lovern! I need to fucking talk to you, and the longer you take, the more you're pissing me the fuck off! Open the door! I don't know who's in there making you believe I'm some kinda sucka, but I'm done playing with you! This is your last chance!" He didn't even believe that I could think for myself. He thought I was in the apartment with some other man, an utterly absurd thought after all Guy had put me through, when all I was trying to do was keep myself safe.

"Please, you know I can't open the door. Just please leave! You're scaring me, Guy! Please!" I begged even louder.

"Don't say I didn't warn you," he muttered angrily. I heard footsteps retreating away from the door. My heart pounded as anxiety surged through me. He warned me. Warned me about what? Whatever he was referring to, I knew it was bad.

I didn't have a peephole on my door to see if he was still lurking in the hallway, and opening the door was not an option. I looked out my window that faced the courtyard of the property just in time to see Guy walking hastily toward the street, around the corner, and out of sight. I paced the bedroom area back and forth in a state of panic, mind racing. I was being held hostage by his intimidation, and didn't know what to do but wait it out. Less than five minutes later, loud footsteps came down the hallway in the direction of my door.

Slam! Slam! Slam! Guy had returned, and it sounded like he was violently pounding his whole body against my door in hopes of breaking in. Thinking fast, I pressed my back up against it.

"Please, please, please! I am begging you to stop this! Please!" I yelled, sobbing and terrified.

"I gave you a chance, but you wouldn't listen when all I wanted to do was talk!"

The banging stopped, replaced by a feverish scraping outside the door.

"Jesus, what are you doing, Guy? I know you don't just wanna talk. You're really scaring me! If you don't stop, I'm gonna have to call the police! Please, just leave! Just leave!" I momentarily left my post at the door to cross the room and grab my landline phone. I wanted him to hear me dial the numbers. "I'm calling the police! You gotta go now! Please!"

Initially, calling the cops was an empty threat that I hoped would scare him off and make it all stop. Even with everything happening, I didn't want to be responsible for Guy going to jail. Over the years, I had come to understand the issues surrounding racism, and had seen men in my current neighborhood wrongfully sent to jail just because of the color of their skin. As a black woman, I did not want to be the reason that another black man ended up in the pipeline. I had already done that with my youngest brother and felt sick about it. As a child, I had seen my mother and other women on our street endure it for years. They were able to keep their partners out of jail during their "husband and wife tiffs." The difference between me and them was that I was done with Guy for good and never, ever going back. I still felt like I should be able to reason with him and avoid dialing the phone.

So I pretended to call the cops, hoping that would be enough to make him leave. With my body once again pressed up against the door, I put the phone to my ear, but heard no dial tone. The phone line was dead!

"You are fucking bluffing, bitch!" Guy yelled.

Slam! Slam! Slam! Slam! He banged his body against the door a few more times, then stopped to scrape again.

My logic about keeping black men out of prison and my instinct to protect him over myself both left my mind completely. In a flash, I realized I simply could not handle any of this on my own anymore.

Think, Lovern! Think! After a minute or so, I remembered my prepaid cell phone. I leaned forward to reach my purse hanging on the outside of my closet door and fished it out. I hit a few buttons before remembering I had no minutes left on it. I always re-upped my credit on the weekends, and I hadn't done it yet that day. *Shit, shit, shit! Could this get any worse?*

I also remembered hearing somewhere in passing that even if you had no minutes, you could still dial emergency numbers. I prayed to God this was true and proceeded to dial 911 as Guy resumed banging on the door with his entire body. I waited, prayed, and waited some more. After what seemed like an eternity, I heard the phone ring. The call seemed to be going through.

"911, what's your emergency?" A female dispatcher picked up. It worked!

"Um, yes! Um, someone is trying to break into my apartment and I need help now. Please send help!" Yes, I said it was *someone*. I didn't name him. This was the way I would let him know that I was done keeping his secret, but not get him in trouble. If he had any sense, he would leave.

"Ma'am, you don't know who this person is?" The dispatcher asked.

"No! Please send help, please hurry!"

"You're bluffing... you ain't talking to nobody!" Guy screamed through the door.

"Where do you live, ma'am?" The dispatcher continued.

"195 Ashmont Street, Apt. D4, Dorchester! Please hurry!"

"Help is on the way, ma'am. Stay on the line with me, help is on the way... I can hear banging noises."

"Yes! They're trying to break the door down! How far are they? Please hurry!"

"The police are close, ma'am, just stay with me, okay?"

"Okay!"

Suddenly, there was silence on the other side of the door. I stopped responding to the dispatcher to try and figure out what this meant.

"Ma'am, are you still there?"

When I answered her, I whispered my response so I could still listen to what was going on, on the other side of the door. Guy may have still been outside, just waiting. "I'm here, but I don't know what's happening. I think they're gone but I'm not sure, and I'm afraid to open the door. How far are the police?" My voice quivered at the thought of what he could be doing outside to make sure he got his hands on me one last time.

"Ma'am, they should be approaching you as we speak, just stay with me, okay?" The dispatcher's voice was reassuring, but time seemed to stand still as I waited, my body still pressed against the door. All I could give her now was more silence.

"Do you live alone, Ma'am?"

Loud, repeated knocks sounded from the other side of the door.

"Boston Police! Open up!" A heavy voice yelled. They were finally here! Or was it still Guy out there, changing his voice to try and get me to open the door?

"How do I know it's you? How do I know you're really the Police?" I had to be sure. There was a pause from the other side as I listened intently for the voice to respond. My cell phone away from my ear, I could hear the dispatcher saying something faintly, but I had to pay attention to the voice at the door.

"I'm putting my badge toward the bottom of the door for you to take a look." This voice did sound different from Guy's. I knelt down on my elbows and knees to look through the crack between the door and floor. Like the voice had promised, there was the badge and it looked real. I also saw his shoes, and they certainly weren't Guy's. I sprung up from the floor, while putting the phone to my ear to let the dispatcher know that I was going to hang up and thanked her. After hanging up, I turned both locks to their open positions.

When I pulled open the door two tall, African American officers in plain clothes stood in front of me. The guns on their waists were visible. It was the first time I had been that close to any kind of firearm and it was a bit daunting. Even so, I was overcome with relief that they had finally showed up, and burst into tears. In reality their response time was only about four minutes, but it had to be the longest four minutes of my entire life.

"Miss, can you tell me your name?"

"Lovern Anderson. My name is Lovern Anderson. See, I tried to call you from my landline but it was dead, so I used my cell phone as the person trying to get in was using something to scrape the door on the outside. Did you see him?"

"Well that explains the wood chippings on the floor out here. They were using something like a crowbar to get in between the lock area." He used his flashlight to illuminate the pile of large paint chips and wood shavings on the floor.

"So before we go any further, my name is Detective Johns and this is Detective Thomas."

The other officer and I nodded at each other in response to Johns' introduction.

"You mentioned your landline was dead? Where are your phone lines located?"

"Oh, I don't know exactly."

"Okay. How can we get to the basement?"

"Those stairs there lead to them." I pointed to the staircase located at the other end of the hallway which was barely used.

Johns told his partner to use that staircase to check the lines, seeming confident they would be there. "Are you sure you don't know who was trying to break into your apartment?" He side-stepped past me gently as he entered my apartment, curiously looking around and pointing his bright flashlight in corners of the bedroom space.

"No, I don't." From the look on the officer's face, I knew he didn't believe me.

"Is there any reason why someone would be trying to harm you, Miss Anderson?" he asked as he continued to prod about my space. He paused, waiting for my answer, and looked out the bedroom window that peered into the courtyard.

My arms folded in defense. It started to feel like I was on trial, and losing the courtroom battle. "No, I…".

Detective Thomas' loud footsteps interrupted me as he returned from the basement and stood in the apartment doorway. "Well, the phone lines were cut down there. Whoever was on the other side of the door was really trying to get to you if they went through the trouble of doing all that."

My arms still folded, I had no response for him.

"Look," Johns continued, "we don't suggest you stay here tonight. Do you have someone you can stay with? It's not safe for you to be here alone." His tone was matter-of-fact, and I knew he was right. My life was playing out like one of the many crime dramas I loved to watch, and I had no control over how the story ended.

"I won't. I'll get some things and go somewhere else tonight."

"Alright. Well, unfortunately there isn't much we can do. We'll check the perimeters and block before we leave. If this person happens to come back, please call 911 again." Johns poked around his flashlight one more time in the direction of the kitchen before he and Detective Thomas made their way to the door.

"I will. Thank you for your help." I watched them walk down the narrow hallway, then retreated into my apartment and locked the door. I watched from the window as they hustled about the courtyard looking around, then onto the curb, around the corner, and out of sight.

If someone you know has asked you for help dealing with or escaping an abusive partner, first, encourage them to reach out to The Hotline via phone or chat, if it's safe, and then, you can call or chat with us too. Our advocates can help you make a safety plan that's customized to your friend or family member's situation, and help you find articles and examples of safety planning to share with your loved one as well. We're here 24/7/365 to help everyone affected by abuse.

Source: *https://www.thehotline.org/resources/ when-a-survivor-asks-you-for-help/*

CHAPTER 14:
The Support Needed

I had told the police I would be staying with someone that night, but in reality I didn't know who I could call. Who would I be able to tell this whole ordeal, ending with, "Can I crash at your place until I feel safe again, which might be a week or longer?" I felt like there was no one, so instead I got my jacket, wallet, and keys and went to the train station next door. I got on the next outbound train and rode it all the way to the end. I knew Guy never rode the subway and wouldn't check for me there. I rode the inbound and outbound lines a few times each way that evening. My hoodie covered my head and half my face so I could sob intermittently without anyone seeing me.

By calling 911, I had finally reached out for the help I never wanted and the attention I wasn't looking for. I was convinced that once those cops left my building, I would become an outcast. What would my neighbors think of me now? This would probably also be the tipping point for building management to evict me. After the last ride, I was all cried out and decided I couldn't keep riding the train line back and forth. I was getting tired, hungry, and overall fed up with everything that had transpired. I was especially fed up knowing that this had all come from simply asking to stop being beaten and demeaned.

I got off at my stop and started cautiously walking back to my building, looking around to make sure Guy's car wasn't parked nearby or that he wasn't waiting for me at the corner. I rounded the bend and approached the stairs to the courtyard where there was a welcoming, familiar face waiting. It was Amanda, my high school friend who lived next door to my building.

"Girl, you okay? I've been waiting for you. I kept calling and you didn't answer. Your cell went straight to voicemail and your house phone kept giving a busy tone. I came by and buzzed your bell, but you never answered. I was worried!"

She continued on to say that she had seen Guy hastily get into his car, which had been parked in front of her apartment on a side street. She became even more worried when she saw the police a short while later. I was stunned that she was privy to all of that, and had connected all of it to me being in trouble. Tears filled my eyes again when I realized how much she cared.

"I am so ashamed, girl. Do you have time to go upstairs, so we can talk more? I don't want my neighbors to come out and see me like this," I said with my head down and tears rolling down my cheeks.

"Of course, yeah, yeah! Let's go!"

I was so relieved she agreed, because it meant I didn't have to go up by myself. We started in the direction of the main entrance to the building, when I stopped suddenly and made her stop, too.

"Actually, I am scared out of my mind to go upstairs. Do you mind if we drive for a little bit, or go somewhere else? If he's somewhere looking at me, he'll see I'm leaving and might get tired of waiting." Telling Amanda this might make her apprehensive as well, but I felt it was important to let her know what was really happening if she was choosing to get involved.

"Um, yeah, sure. Walk with me, I'm parked right around the corner. "

Amanda and I had become friends during our senior year of high school in the States. When she moved into the same area I lived in, it felt good to know she was close by. She had seen Guy with me a few times, and witnessed him yelling at me from her window while we were seated in his car in front of her apartment. Without knowing the full scope of what I experienced behind closed doors, she had told me I could call her if I ever needed anything. I never had before, but the care and concern in her voice on this night told me I could trust her.

We got into her car and she drove to a nearby park. After she parked, I gushed like a river about all the details that led to the police coming by that afternoon. Her eyes widened as I told her about the ordeal that sent me to the hospital. She held my hand and rubbed my back as I tearfully recounted all that had happened. She was in disbelief and it showed as she cried along with me. She listened and listened and listened some more, adding her input here and there. Hours passed as we sat talking in her car.

"What do you wanna do? It's clearly not safe for you to be at your place," Amanda surmised.

"I know, but after talking it out with you, I really don't believe Guy's gonna come back tonight, knowing I could call the police at any time if he tries. He's upping his tactics, but so am I. I don't think he's that stupid. Do you think you can stay with me? Just for tonight? I understand if you can't. You've done enough already and I appreciate you for that."

"I can stay, don't worry about it. We'll Cagney and Lacey his ass if he decides to show up!" That comment made us both laugh out loud.

"Only if I can be Lacey," I said good-naturedly. It felt good to finally have someone in my corner who wasn't judging me.

We headed back to her place where she grabbed some things, including her can of mace, and we headed to my apartment where she spent the night. I had her help me push the dresser back in front of the door, but Guy did not show up or attempt to call.

Though we succeeded in making my apartment feel safe that first night, I was still scared to be alone in the days following. Amanda came over almost every day and stayed with me for hours, just listening as I unloaded about all that had happened to me in that tiny studio apartment. When she couldn't come over, she called to check in and listened from home. While her anger toward Guy was mixed with disbelief, she always alluded to the fact that I was the one in control now and that it took a lot of strength to make the move to speak up. It meant the world to me that she didn't condemn me for staying with him as long as I did. Amanda had viewed me as smart and independent prior to ever meeting Guy, and she believed that was still who I was. This reassurance empowered me to move forward without thinking of going back. It meant everything that my friend believed in me.

Stalking generally refers to harassing or threatening behavior that an individual engages in repeatedly, such as following a person, appearing at a person's home or place of business, making harassing phone calls, leaving written messages or objects, or vandalizing a person's property. These actions may or may not be accompanied by a credible threat of serious harm, and they may or may not be precursors to an assault or murder. If you believe you are experiencing stalking, document as much about the behaviors in question as possible to create evidence of a pattern of a behavior, which can be helpful when making a report to law enforcement.

Source: *https://www.thehotline.org/resources/stalking-safety-planning/*

CHAPTER 15:
Leave Me Alone

About two weeks had passed since Guy had shown up at the apartment and tried to break down the door. I could no longer use the amount of time gone by as a barometer of whether he was going to show up again, because that failed me miserably last time. I made myself even more scarce around the apartment building, assuming word had traveled that the black girl in apartment D4 had a man that beat on her, so she had to call the cops on him. Every day I believed that the call from building management was going to come, or that I would come home to find a note from them posted to my door or in my mailbox telling me I was evicted. My level of shame and embarrassment was at an all time high.

Amanda became my real MVP during this time. She was now taking the train to work and letting me use her car while I shopped for my own. Walking back and forth from the train station had become impossible with the thought that Guy could be lurking in some corner. Since I had called the cops on him, that was a very real fear. Despite her "screw him" attitude, Amanda also feared for me and didn't want me taking any chances. Lending me her car was a huge gesture that I am still very grateful for.

I looked over my shoulder wherever I went. My guard was always up, and it turned out my fears were warranted. One morning around 7am, after double-checking that Guy was not lingering in the courtyard, I walked out to the sidewalk and rounded the bend to the side street where I parked Amanda's car each evening. As I got closer to it, I noticed there was a piece of white paper on the windshield. I thought it might be a flyer from the church nearby or a fast food advertisement, but when I got closer to the car, I saw it was neither. I lifted the wiper that affixed the note and I was mortified when I read what it said: *You used to say this dick was all you ever needed. You lied bitch!*

Affixed to the paper was a picture of Guy and I on one of our dates early on in the relationship. This meant he had been here and knew I was driving Amanda's car. He had been watching me! I quickly scanned the area around me and saw no sign of him. I walked gingerly around the car to see if he was hidden by one of the doors. He wasn't. I took the paper and picture off the windshield, unlocked the car, put my bag on the passenger side seat, and drove out of there as fast as I could.

When I got to the stoplight, I called Amanda and left a message asking her to meet me on her street that evening when I got home. I didn't go into details so she wouldn't worry. Before the light turned green, I looked over at the picture and note on the passenger seat. *He's hurt that I'm not giving him a chance to try again*, I thought. I was scared by it but also felt a little sorry for the way I had been treating him. Could I have been overreacting? Maybe I should let him know that I still cared about him, but that I just couldn't be with him anymore.

No, Lovern! Get a freaking grip! I knew I had to stay the course, because like Ms. Tina inferred in her song, "love ain't got nothing to do with it" when you'd been through what I'd been through. *Just stay the course*, I kept telling myself.

I pulled into the parking lot of work that morning and composed myself before heading in, just as I had done so many times before. At lunch, I opted to ask my colleagues to bring something back for me as opposed to taking my usual walk with them, and ate in the break room. I was safe inside the office. He couldn't get to me there.

Once the work day was over, I walked out with my colleagues to the parking lot and headed home. Amanda had left me a voicemail during the day saying that she would look out for me and sure enough, she came out of her apartment as I parked the car on her street.

"Everything alright? Why did you want me to meet you out here?" she asked.

"I'm okay, but Guy came early this morning and left these." I fished the note and picture out of my bag and handed them to her. "He left them on the windshield, Amanda!"

"He is tripping Lovern. What the hell? He knows you involved the cops now but who knows what he's gonna do if he's feeling slighted! I think you need to get a restraining order. Who knows what else he'll try? He wants you to know he's pissed that you left him."

I thought a restraining order was a little extreme. Plus, I didn't want to have to deal with the court system and disclose all that had transpired to anyone else. After finding two more notes on Amanda's windshield that week, I quickly changed my mind.

The first read, *Anybody that fucks Lovern is getting sloppy seconds 'cause I had her first!* The handwriting looked like that of a child, but my stomach twisted into knots because I knew it was him.

The next read, *You'll never get another man like me, you bitch!*

I hastily grabbed the notes off the car both times, looking around to see if he was lurking nearby or if anyone else was watching me. Who else had seen these vulgar and demeaning notes as they walked by the car? The tone of each note was angrier than the last, and I knew they would keep getting worse if I didn't once again seek the help that I dreaded. At that point, I knew what Guy was doing put *him* in the wrong, not me. I didn't deserve any of this, so I was going to make it stop.

I called work and said that I felt sick and needed to take the day. I then called the non-emergency line for the police to ask how I would go about obtaining a restraining order. They told me I would have to go to the courthouse and visit the clerk's office to fill one out. Upon arrival, I passed through the metal detectors and followed signs to the clerk's office. I told an available clerk that I was there to file a restraining order and she immediately reached under the counter and handed me the necessary paperwork to fill out. Reading the word "abuse" at the top of the page in relation to my own situation felt surreal.

After filling out the initial form I had to fill out an affidavit, which asks you to plead your case as to why you need a restraining order in writing. I again felt vulnerable, having to open up about the details that led me here. Intimate details about how he always seemed to be lurking, and my never being sure if he would go back to physically hurting me or worse. Who was going to read what I had written here? Would they see me as weak and laugh at me behind closed doors? Even with these negative possibilities, I knew there was no turning back now if I wanted to ever feel secure again. I took my completed forms to the clerk's counter, and she pointed me to one of the courtrooms where I would have to wait to go before the judge.

"Wait, so I have to talk to a judge in front of the whole courtroom about this?" I said in disbelief.

"If you want this order, yes ma'am. Have a seat in there and they'll call your name." She said as she stamped the papers I had just given to her.

I was under that impression they would read what I had given them and decide if I got the order or not, then mail it to me after letting Guy know he had to stay away from me. I was 23 years old and had never set foot inside a courtroom; I didn't have a clue how all this worked. Nevertheless, I did as I was told and headed to the courtroom where I prayed no one I knew would be in there. Entering that room alone was daunting. What was I supposed to do when my name was called? Did I need a lawyer? I wished I had someone there to walk me through the process.

Upon being seated, I realized there were already cases being heard and people were being called to step up into an enclosed box area to speak to the judge. Some had lawyers in tow, others didn't. As I waited my turn, I heard a couple of other cases related to abuse orders, but from what I deduced, they were for men who had violated their restraining orders and would be going to jail because of it. The women who were there seeking help described the horror they went through from the men who disregarded their orders. As I listened to them, I began to think Guy would probably disregard my order too, out of rage after being served with papers. *What the hell am I doing here? I could end up dead! I should just leave because he'll come after me anyway!* I thought in despair.

"....Anderson? Lovern Anderson!"

I quickly put my thoughts to the side and stood up, my hand raised in response. The person who had yelled my name asked me to step into the boxed-in area facing the judge. I stood there as someone else handed the judge what I assumed were the forms I'd filled out earlier. A third person explained something to the judge, but their words were a blur as my head spun with hundreds of thoughts all at once.

"Ms. Anderson, can you tell me why you feel like you're in danger?" asked the judge.

'Ummm, well… as I noted in my affidavit, Judge, I have been afraid, looking over my shoulder, everywhere I go because *this guy* has been popping up everywhere. He leaves derogatory notes on my car and has tried to break into my apartment, ever since I told him I didn't want to be with him anymore." I started to cry as I spoke. "I'm afraid he's going to come after me in public. He has in the past."

As I spoke, the courtroom seemed to get much more silent than it had been while I waited to go up. I felt everyone's eyes on me. All of these people were seeing me as weak. My stomach twisted in tight knots as I tried to read the faces of the courtroom workers in front of me as well as the judge's. It was humiliating having to repeat everything I'd thought I could keep private and deal with on my own.

"Thank you, Ms. Anderson. You are being granted a Ten Day Temporary Order. We will set this for 10 days from now and see you back here for the hearing," the judge said as he wrote on the paperwork and handed it to his nearby bailiff.

Wait, what? What did he mean, he would see me in ten days? I thought in a panic. *I thought we just had the hearing! And, I only get it for ten days?* I thought I would get at least a year of protection right then and there.

"Uh, okay, thank you." It all moved so quickly, I didn't feel like I had the right to ask the judge for clarity.

Frustrated, I stepped back, gathered my things from my seat I had sat in earlier, and turned to exit the courtroom. As I power-walked to the door, I felt a slight tug on my purse. I looked down to my right to see an African American, grey haired, wide-eyed woman looking up at me.

"You gonna be alright, young lady. Keep your head up, you hear me?" she whispered beneath the sounds of the courtroom worker calling for the next person's case.

"Thank you. I will." I touched her hand to extend further thanks for her sentiments, and continued toward the exit. I was reassured to know at least one person in the courtroom saw me as strong.

I headed straight to the clerk's office to get an explanation about the judge's instructions. The same woman who had helped me earlier was still at the counter. After I told her why I was confused, she explained that the ten days gives the person you are accusing time to be notified that they have to show up for the final hearing, and that Guy may or may not be there on that day. She further explained that if he did appear for that hearing, he would have a chance to voice his side and the judge would decide if I would be granted a year of protection.

This is just freaking great, I thought sarcastically. Going through this piece alone had been brutal enough, and now I might have to face him, too? I'd also have to take another day off work under the pretense that I was sick. *Just great.*

I went home that day feeling completely drained. I did nothing for the rest of the day but process what had happened in court. No tears came that afternoon, just fear and confusion about what would happen in ten days. Time slowed to a crawl in anticipation of the next court date and I stayed vigilant everywhere I went, always wondering if this was the day he would lash out against my latest attempt to protect myself.

***

When the day of the hearing arrived, I entered the courthouse early. I went into the clerk's office and was told to go to the same courtroom I had appeared in the last time. When I turned in the direction I needed to go, I noticed Guy pacing back and forth outside the courtroom's door.

The sight of him stopped me in my tracks. I was petrified. For a second I thought about turning around and going back into the office to hide until the session started since I didn't think he had seen me. Then remembered that if I did, I would not be able to hear my name when my case was called. I started to walk slowly in his direction and about ten steps in, our eyes locked. His were filled with pure rage. Just then, the court officer poked his head into the hallway to announce that the session was about to begin. Guy quickly headed in behind him, but not before he looked in my direction one more time.

I took my time walking in. Upon entering, I scanned the room and saw Guy sitting on the left side close to the center, so I took a seat at the back right corner. My heart was racing. I was safe here now, but what about after court adjourned?

"All rise!" the courtroom officer yelled. The whole room stood up as the judge came in and got seated. "Docket number…" The officer read on, rattling off a string of numbers before reading my and Guy's names. Our case was first.

I got up and came to the front of the boxed-in area on my side of the room. Guy did the same on his side. I could feel his eyes glaring at me. There was nothing between us except space, and I pictured him lunging at me in rage. I was shaking. The officer swore us in to tell the truth, the whole truth, and nothing but the truth. Guy was so good at blaming me for everything in the relationship, it would be interesting to hear what he would present as the truth that morning.

"Ms. Anderson, do you need a minute? Are you okay to proceed?" The judge asked when he saw my discomfort.

"Yes, but can I have a tissue please?" The courtroom officer passed several to me as I sought to regain my composure.

"Ms. Anderson, can you state why you believe you are in danger?" asked the judge.

"Um, do you want me to repeat what I said the last time I was here?"

"Yes, please state it for the court."

Voice shaking, tears streaming, I began to repeat parts of my restraining order's affidavit section, making sure to reference the vile notes he had left on the car. When I was through, the judge asked Guy whether or not what I had said was true.

"Look Judge, I mean, I was with her for a bit, but she had been seeing other men while we were together. I have never seen these notes she says I wrote before in my life. I mean, it actually looks like a kid wrote them. Maybe it was one of them illiterate fools she's been sleeping around with that put 'em there. It wasn't me. I moved on and she's delusional. She's never been a trustworthy person, Judge. I don't even know why I'm here. I mean the men she's been with, it could be any one of them."

I was dumbfounded. Would the judge believe any of this? Guy and I had now each said our piece, and there was nothing I could do but wait as the judge sifted through papers and considered our words.

"The court is going to issue a one year protection order to Ms. Anderson after finding she has borne the burden of proof. Sir, you are not to come within one hundred yards of Ms. Anderson or the addresses listed on the

Restraining Order filed after stalking activity:

ABUSE PREVENTION ORDER (G.L. c. 209A) Page 1 of 2	DOCKET NO. ███████ (AR)	TRIAL COURT OF MASSACHUSETTS

PLAINTIFF'S NAME **Lovern** ██████	Defendant's Name and ████ ██████████	Alias, if any	n/a

NAME & ADDRESS OF COURT	D E F T. I N F O.	Date of Birth	Place of Birth
Dorchester District Court 510 Washington Street Dorchester, MA. 02124		SS # ██████████	Daytime Phone # (
	Sex [X] M [ ] F Mother's Maiden Name (First & Last)		
	Father's Name (First & Last)		

VIOLATION OF THIS ORDER IS A CRIMINAL OFFENSE punishable by imprisonment or fine or both.

A. THE COURT HAS ISSUED THE FOLLOWING ORDERS TO THE DEFENDANT: (only those items checked shall apply)

[ ] This Order was issued without advance notice because the Court determined that there is a substantial likelihood of immediate danger of abuse.   [ ] This Order was communicated by telephone from the Judge named below to: Police Dept._____ Police Officer_____

[X] **1. YOU ARE ORDERED NOT TO ABUSE THE PLAINTIFF** by harming, threatening or attempting to harm the Plaintiff physically or by placing the Plaintiff in fear of imminent serious physical harm, or by using force, threat or duress to make the Plaintiff engage in sexual relations unwillingly.

[X] **2. YOU ARE ORDERED NOT TO CONTACT THE PLAINTIFF,** except as permitted in 8 below or for notification of court proceedings as permitted in this section, either in person, by telephone, in writing or otherwise, either directly or through someone else, and to stay at least 100 yards from the Plaintiff even if the Plaintiff seems to allow or request contact. Notification of court proceedings is permissible only by mail, or by sheriff or other authorized officer when required by statute or rule.

[X] **3. YOU ARE ORDERED TO IMMEDIATELY LEAVE AND STAY AWAY FROM THE PLAINTIFF'S RESIDENCE,** except as permitted in 8 below, located at **195 Ashmont St.#D4 Dorch.** _____or wherever else you may have reason to know the Plaintiff may reside. The Court also **ORDERS** you to (a) to surrender any keys to that residence to the Plaintiff, (b) not to damage any belongings of the Plaintiff or any other occupant, (c) not to shut off or cause to be shut off any utilities or mail delivery to the Plaintiff, and (d) not to interfere in any way with the Plaintiff's right to possess that residence, except by appropriate legal proceedings.

[X] If this box is checked, the Court also **ORDERS** you to immediately leave and remain away from the entire apartment building or other multiple family dwelling in which the Plaintiff's residence is located.

[ ] **4. PLAINTIFF'S ADDRESS IMPOUNDED.** The Court ORDERS that the address of the Plaintiff's residence is to be impounded by the Clerk-Magistrate or Register of Probate so that it is not disclosed to you, your attorney, or the public.

[X] **5. YOU ARE ORDERED TO STAY AWAY FROM THE PLAINTIFF'S WORKPLACE** located at ██████████ Boston

[ ] **6. CUSTODY OF THE FOLLOWING CHILDREN IS AWARDED TO THE PLAINTIFF:**

NAME	DOB	NAME	DOB

[ ] **7. YOU ARE ORDERED NOT TO CONTACT THE CHILDREN LISTED ABOVE OR ANY CHILDREN IN THE PLAINTIFF'S CUSTODY LISTED BELOW,** either in person, by telephone, in writing or otherwise, either directly or through someone else, and to stay at least _____ yards away from them unless you receive written permission from the Court to do otherwise.
[ ] You are also ordered to stay away from the following school, day care, other: _____

NAME	DOB	NAME	DOB

[ ] **8. VISITATION WITH THE CHILDREN LISTED IN SECTION 6 IS PERMITTED ONLY AS FOLLOWS** (may be ordered by Probate and Family Court only): _____

[ ] Visitation is only allowed if supervised and in the presence of _____ at the following times _____ to be paid for by _____
[ ] Transportation of children to and from this visitation is to be done by _____ (third party), and not by you.
[ ] You may contact the Plaintiff by telephone only to arrange this visitation.

[ ] **9. YOU ARE ORDERED TO PAY SUPPORT** for [ ] the Plaintiff and [ ] your child or children listed above, at the rate of $_____ per [ ] week or per _____, beginning _____, 199___ [ ] directly to the Plaintiff [ ] through the Probation Office of this Court [ ] through the Massachusetts Department of Revenue [ ] by income assignment.

[ ] **10. YOU MAY PICK UP YOUR PERSONAL BELONGINGS** in the company of police at a time agreed by the Plaintiff.

[ ] **11. YOU ARE ORDERED TO COMPENSATE THE PLAINTIFF** for $_____ in losses suffered as a direct result of the abuse, to be paid in full on or before _____, 199___ [ ] directly to the Plaintiff [ ] through the Probation Office of this Court.

[X] **12. THERE IS A SUBSTANTIAL LIKELIHOOD OF IMMEDIATE DANGER OF ABUSE. YOU ARE ORDERED TO IMMEDIATELY SURRENDER** to the **Boston C-11** _____ Police Department all guns, ammunition, gun licenses and FID cards. Your license to carry a gun, if any, and your FID card, if any, are suspended immediately.
► You may ask the Court to change this Order by going to the Court and filing a petition. The Court will schedule a hearing on your petition.
► You must immediately surrender the items listed above, and also comply with all other Orders in this case, whether or not you file a petition.
► If you need a firearm, rifle, shotgun, machine gun, or ammunition for your job, you may ask for a hearing within two days.

[X] **13. YOU ARE ALSO ORDERED** *to stay away for* ████████████ *and* ████████████

The Plaintiff must appear at scheduled hearings, or this Order may be vacated. The Defendant may appear, with or without attorney, to oppose any extension or modification of this Order. If the Defendant does not appear, this Order may be extended or modified as determined by the Judge. For good cause, either the Plaintiff or the Defendant may request the Court to modify this Order before its scheduled expiration date.

FA 2 (9/95)

Excerpt from Restraining Order

I HAVE DECIDED TO GET THIS ORDER AGAINST
tIM. I'VE known THE DEFENDANT FOR
1 YEAR AND 8 MONTHS. DURING THE COURSE OF
THE RELATIONSHIP, ABUSE WAS PRESENT, EVER MORE
SO WHEN I DECIDED TO END IT. I HAD PREVIOUS

order. A copy of the order will be provided to you both at the clerk's office. Do either of you have any questions?"

"No. Um, thank you, Honor." I responded gratefully, a wave of relief flowing through my body. I don't remember if Guy said anything in response; I was too overcome by the feeling that I finally had some level of control over my life.

The judge dismissed us, and I headed back to my seat to leisurely gather my things, moving slowly on purpose in the hopes that Guy would exit before me. I finally watched him walk past my seat. He glanced in my direction, giving me one more foul look as he did. I had rattled the hornet's nest. The question now was whether he would make me pay, or adhere to the order that the judge passed. Affidavit filed.

Abuse is a learned behavior. Some people witness it in their own families growing up; others learn it slowly from friends, popular culture, or structural inequities throughout our society. No matter where they develop such behaviors, those who commit abusive acts make a choice in doing so — they also could choose not to.

There are many people who experience or witness abuse who use their experiences to end the cycle of violence and heal themselves without harming others. While outside factors (including drug or alcohol addiction) can escalate abuse, it's important to recognize that these issues do not cause domestic abuse themselves.

Source: *National Domestic Violence Hotline*

It is natural for survivors to feel fear and regret from time to time. Looking ahead will give them hope. It is usually best for survivors to separate themselves as much as possible from the controlling person and his contacts, so they cannot be controlled or monitored through someone else.

Source: *www.psychologytoday.com/us/blog/invisible-chains/201512/ recovery-after-controlling-relationship*

CHAPTER 16:
Picking Up The Pieces

Guy's pattern of stalking ceased after the restraining order was issued. A few months after the court date my guard was still completely up, to the point of adding a self-imposed nightly curfew. I wanted to regain a sense of normalcy, but I was also mourning the loss of the relationship. I ragged on myself mentally for not being able to fix him and eventually make the relationship work. I had excelled in many areas of life, but couldn't stop a man from beating on me. I felt like a failure.

The friends I had known from high school in the States were in their second year of college and some of them were still dating the same guys from back then. Some had new guys, and many were engaged to be married. Amanda, my dear friend who helped me navigate leaving Guy, got a new job in another state and moved away.

Then there was me, the 23-year-old trying to repair a life that had fallen to shambles. I had gotten my own car which made life much more convenient, but I still felt like a wreck emotionally and mentally. I was down, depressed, and unsure of myself all the time. If I was at the grocery store or another public setting, I was leery of men looking at me or paying me compliments, because Guy had taught me that they always had ulterior motives. I would try my best to not make eye contact with them, because I viewed myself as damaged goods. The whole Guy-withdrawal process was full of self loathing and insecurity.

One Saturday afternoon as I sat around watching TV, an advertisement for the local The New England Institute of Art caught my attention. I was intrigued that one of their offerings was TV/Broadcasting. *I could be a reporter*, I thought. I spoke articulately, looked the part, and had a great personality. I reminded myself that I was all those things before meeting Guy. I was interested in learning more, so I started looking into the program.

Around that same time, I had reached out to Mummy who was really glad to hear from me. She was even more glad that I had broken up with Guy. I refrained from going into detail about the hell he had put me through and focused on setting up a time for her to finally visit my apartment. I slowly started reconnecting with other family members as well, including my younger brothers Sean and Javan. Everyone welcomed me back with open arms.

One day at the store, I ran into my high school best friend, Debbie. We had not been in contact for the majority of the past two years, and we were excited to see each other. We chatted for a little bit and she invited me to her church, which wasn't too far from where I lived. I accepted and we exchanged numbers before going our separate ways. It felt good that I didn't have to rush the conversation or be concerned that I was going over my allotted time running an errand.

I met Debbie at her church the following Sunday to attend service. I fully enjoyed the Praise and Worship portion; it was just what I needed to open myself up to the sermon about to be delivered. Have you ever been to church and felt like the pastor was talking directly to you as they preached? That was me that morning. The sermon about God's unconditional love for us is one I will never forget.

After speaking for a bit, the pastor asked everyone to go to Colossians: Chapter 3, Verse 12 in our Bibles which read: *Therefore, as God's chosen people, holy and dearly loved, clothe yourselves with compassion, kindness, humility, gentleness, and patience.* He explained that we tend to focus on the things we lack but in reality, we each are enough just the way we are, with nothing added or taken away. He continued that we needed to take time with ourselves, just as God takes time with us each and every day.

Those sentiments really resonated with me. In that moment, I fully recognized that I was a whole and complete person before I met *this guy*. I never asked to be abused and I sure as hell didn't do it to myself. I needed to be more gentle and kind to myself. I needed to show myself more compassion. The Bible verse eluded to how much God loved us—how much He loved *me*—and I needed to lean into that omni-present love a little more.

I hugged my friend at the end of service and promised I would return the following Sunday. From there on, I found myself attending service almost every Sunday, mostly looking forward to Praise and Worship and the pastor's sermon. Each time I left the building, I felt optimistic about the week ahead. I started praying intermittently throughout the day. My prayers always related to giving thanks for sparing my life and for placing people on my path to help me along the way. I was not a devout Christian at this point, but returning to the basic principles I had learned attending church when I was younger felt great.

I joined a local gym where I mostly ran on the treadmill to clear my mind. I started going out with Debbie a little more, and reconnecting with other old friends as well. As the days and months passed by, I found the fear and dread slowly retreating from the front of my mind. This was also apparent in my journal entries that began shortly after the restraining order. After a few months my writing went from dark to light.

Later that year, I decided to leave the company where I had worked during my escape from *that guy*, and took a part-time secretarial job that paid decent money. I did this so I could follow through with applying for the fall semester at The New England Institute of Art to attend class full-time during the day. I was set on giving this new dream of becoming a reporter an honest attempt. After being accepted to the program, I worked hard and loved every minute of it. In my senior year, I landed an internship at the local affiliate for Fox News. I was having the time of my life going to school, making new friends and interning at one of the top local news stations. Everything in my life was shifting in a positive direction. The sky was the limit.

After I graduated with my degree, I took a chance to apply for an open entry-level position in the station's Traffic Department. No, it wasn't a job monitoring automobile crashes from a helicopter. In this context, "traffic" referred to the station's flow of commercial breaks during the day. I got the job and the day I was hired, I cried with happiness.

About a year after being hired, I was promoted within the department to a senior role. On my own time, I started seeking help to make a reporter's demo reel that would help me apply for reporter positions down the road. I had developed more than a few great relationships with seasoned reporters and photographers on staff, who helped me compile one by letting me do ride-alongs to new stories they were covering. I completed it with coaching from a couple of the morning anchors, who directed my anchor desk video.

Lovern Augustine
2004

Traffic Coordinator
FOX25 News

choose a reputable
internship

**New England Institute of
Art Alumni Hall Feature**

Now at 26 years old, my next goal was to buy my first home closer to work. After a rigorous bank loan process, I was successful! I invited my mom to live with me so she didn't have to keep paying high rent or working as hard as she did.

With my demo reel complete and house purchased, I was ready to apply for reporter positions. It was around that time I found out that I would have to start out in a lower news market out of state. I learned that the chances of me getting a job in the Boston market without experience were slim to none. I was crushed, because it just wasn't feasible to leave and start over in a new market now that I had a mortgage. I resigned myself to focusing on perfecting my skills just in case a reporter gig opened up at one of the smaller stations locally.

In 2009, everyone was feeling the strain of the recession that started the prior year. It hit the news industry in the form of a lack of advertising sales. One day, a couple of folks from other departments came to ours to say that they were just laid off after being with the station for a very long time. Our work area was always seen as a safe space to come for lighthearted chat, but that day it was consumed with despair after this sudden news was delivered. My laid-off coworkers couldn't do much more than cry shocked, hurt tears.

The next few days were filled with a high level of job uncertainty and it was scary for everyone, not knowing if they would come into work one day just to be told it was their last. I had a mortgage and was repaying school loans. I couldn't risk losing my job with nothing solid to fall back on. I didn't have years of seniority like some of my coworkers, and didn't know what the hire-ups criteria was for laying staff off. As much as I felt at home in the TV industry and as happy as I was working with my team, I needed to decide where I would go from here before they had a chance to lay me off.

One Saturday afternoon, I met up with a girlfriend of mine to see a matinee. There were only select movie theaters showing the particular movie we wanted to see, and the closest one was located a little outside Boston. We took the train to get there, and on the ride I happened to run into my former boss from the company I'd worked for while I was with *that guy*. We were both surprised to see each other and started catching up.

"I'd like to come back and work for you," I somehow managed to blurt out. I figured it couldn't hurt to put this out there, since I needed a change and this opportunity seemed meant to be.

"You would?" she asked, surprised.

"Yes, if you'll have me," I replied with a big smile.

"...stop approaching." The overhead train announcement was loud and cut her off from responding right away. I didn't catch which stop the voice said we were coming to, but apparently it was hers.

"Okay, well this is me, but stop by the office on Wednesday and let's talk more," she said as the doors opened up.

"Yes! I'll definitely be there!" We embraced in a quick hug before she exited the train doors.

That Wednesday, I took the afternoon off at the TV station and went to see my former boss at the new office location. I walked out with a rehire date three weeks from then. I was ecstatic to have this safety net in place. It was hard leaving the news industry, but necessary at the time. In the coming weeks, I wrapped up my stint at the station and switched back to the leasing and finance world in September 2009. My professional life had all come full circle, and yet another shift was still on the horizon.

"When you lose someone you loved at one time, or even still love, but were abused by, you may grieve for the time lost — precious years of your life spent in the abusive relationship," Stern explains. *"You may grieve for your former 'self' in hindsight, now that you are stronger, more optimistic, more open. And you may grieve for the fact that you are forever changed by that relationship."*

Source: *https://www.allure.com/story/grieving-abuser-death*

CHAPTER 17:
The End of An Era

My father, Lloydie, passed away from kidney and liver failure alone in a hospital room in Trinidad. It was April 2002 and he was 50 years old. I had just escaped Guy's abuse the year prior. By 2001, my mother had finally had enough of his long distance lies and believed he was seeing another woman, something her friends from our old neighborhood had been telling her for some time. She was hurt, but too busy with her progressing career to dwell on it. Even though Lloydie and Mummy were still married and communicated amicably, my mother was finally coming into her own as an individual. She had worked her way up to becoming a Certified Nursing Assistant at the well-known rehabilitation hospital where she had started out in the kitchen. I was incredibly proud of her.

Early in 2002, Lloydie began to get sick. His knees mysteriously swelled and he experienced extreme fatigue. My oldest brother Bronson had rushed him to the hospital on several occasions. The last time he went to the emergency room, the staff admitted him because of how quickly he was deteriorating.

In his last week of life, Mummy and I called the phone in his hospital room. During that call, he asked her to consider organizing a flight to the States for him to receive better medical treatment. Mummy was a bit reluctant after all he had put her through, but she obliged. He also asked me to accompany Mummy to Trinidad if anything happened to him, so I could help her with paperwork related to the houses we owned and money he had stored in different banking institutions. I also obliged, but it was eerie to think about.

That phone call was the third time in my entire life that I had spoken one-on-one with my father, and this was by far the most vulnerable he had ever been. This man had possessed so much brute strength and power over us for so many years, and for even more years over Mummy, but he sounded so weak and powerless over the phone. I had never seen him seek medical attention in my entire life, and now he was at the mercy of nurses for everything from administering medication to helping him get to the bathroom. I couldn't picture it.

Later that week, Mummy called to let him know she had found a flight and was ready to finalize details. A nurse answered the phone to let her know that Lloydie had passed away that morning. Mummy called me and asked me to come over so she could tell me the news, but her tone of voice worried me enough that I begged her to tell me right then. When she did, I couldn't believe it. We had just spoken to him earlier in the week and now, just like that, he was gone.

There was a part of me that hoped to become better acquainted with the vulnerable voice I had heard on the phone when he came to Massachusetts for dialysis treatment. Maybe we could have had some semblance of a normal father-daughter relationship.

Mummy and I flew to Trinidad the following week to arrange his funeral. By the time we arrived, the word of his passing had spread quickly throughout the neighborhood. Many of our old neighbors were as shocked as we were.

The day of the funeral, I took a minute to view Lloydie in his casket. It finally sank in that he was really gone. I took my seat next to my Mummy at the front of the overcrowded funeral parlor. The attendance showed me how well-known and liked he was by his peers.

It was my job to read his eulogy, which I had written off the cuff a couple of hours before. Aside from our strained relationship, what made this difficult was that Lloydie had told us so little so little about his life over the years. What do you say about a man you hardly knew? I was able to do a decent job with the facts I had, including his academic and professional accomplishments. Some tears spilled from my eyes as I delivered the speech, but they didn't start flowing heavily until the crowd congregated at the burial site and a pastor cousin read his last rights. I was overcome with grief as my father's casket was lowered into the ground. My limbs became weak and I was shaking a little. I wore shades on this sunny afternoon to protect my eyes, but they ended up catching the pool of water that ran out of my eyes as the casket got lower and lower.

How in the world could I feel this immense amount of sadness over someone who had caused so much harm to my mother? Someone who never cared about his family's well-being? How could I now be grieving this callous soul? I couldn't explain the immense amount of sadness I felt.

Watching my mother sob, I seemed to understand her tears. For over 30 years, so much of her identity was wrapped up in this person who was now being placed in the ground before her. Even though she had recently begun to forge her own way in the world, it would take a lifetime to fall out of love with him.

Bron's tears also had me tied up in knots. I had never seen him cry, but here he was, weeping over the man who used to beat him like a dog. His convenience shop business had grown over the years, and while he was still full of the anger from our childhood, he had learned to manage it while serving customers from sun-up to sun-down with a high level of Obsessive Compulsive Disorder (OCD). Some symptoms of this disorder in his case were needing things to be perfectly symmetrical, cleaning both himself and his surrounding environment obsessively, and having disturbing intrusive thoughts that caused him to talk quietly to himself. I came to understand many years later that these behaviors were because of the abuse he witnessed and received. He had grown up defending himself from Lloydie, and then continued to defend our mother against him as an adult living next door. Now, here he was, moved to tears over the same man.

Lloydie's reign of power and control was no more. His casket now fully in its resting place, dirt was shoveled on top to bury this chapter of our lives forever.

CHAPTER 18:
I Dare You!

By 2010, I was a fully reintegrated social butterfly with a mix of different friends outside of work. I was wide open to experiencing new things and loved meeting new people. My appetite for life was big, partially because my father's passing showed me that tomorrow isn't promised. One of the many things I did regularly was a quarterly girls night with a group of girlfriends. During one of these nights, my friend Janelle mentioned that she was excited about a pageant system called the Ethnic New England Pageant that she was about to introduce in the Boston area. It would be a different type of beauty pageant, where the swimsuit competition was replaced by a category focusing on what was unique about the contestant's ethnicity. We all loved the idea and rooted for her in excitement.

"Lovern, you should take part in it! You'd be great with your little tiny self," one of the other girls shouted. Others joined in loud agreement.

"Y'all are crazy! No, I'm all set," I replied.

"Girl, why not? You too scared to fall in heels on stage or something?" Another friend added in jest. This question made us all erupt in laughter.

"Uh, no! It's just not for me," I replied after catching my breath, a grin still on my face.

"What? You, too, chicken girl... Do it! I dare you!" someone else exclaimed.

"Oh don't dare me, cause I ain't scared of nothin'! Your girl can walk in some heels, okay! Janelle, send me more info later about how I sign up. Count me in!"

The pageant itself was set to happen about a month from that night. I was joining the process quite late in the game, but was dedicated to proving my friends wrong. I reached out to a family friend who was a seamstress to make an evening gown, an ethnic-focused fashion piece, and a sporty uniform for the competition. I took no other measures to prepare because based on what I had seen on TV, a pageant was a piece of cake. I would get through it and have fun, without falling. Simple as that.

A couple of days prior to the event, Janelle and her team members hosted a run-through of the show. This included what to expect that night, walking directions, and meeting the other contestants. Again, piece of cake!

The day of the pageant arrived. It was held at a local college on a clear spring day, and my spirits were high. I had chosen a skirt suit with a blazer for the one-on-one interview round of the competition. I was ready to smile, make eye contact, remain poised, and be precise with my answers to the judges' questions.

I walked into the interview room to a panel of judges made up of two casually well-dressed older gentlemen and two beautiful, poised, and regal older women. I greeted them as I walked in and took my seat in front of them. Nerves set in that I hadn't felt earlier in the process, partially because I couldn't read any of the judges' faces or tell whether they liked me. Legs crossed at the feet, palms resting on my lap one on top of the other, I smiled nice and wide. Butterflies swarmed in my stomach. I hoped and prayed my anxiety wasn't visible on the outside.

"Hello, Ms. Anderson," said one of the women as the other judges glanced at me and straightened papers in front of them.

"Good afternoon. Nice to meet you all," I responded shakily. After hearing my voice, I knew my nerves had to be apparent to the panel.

"No need to be nervous, we won't bite," said the other woman, smiling kindly. The sentiment made me feel a little better.

The panel asked some getting-to-know-you questions which were easy enough, and helped me get more comfortable. Then, one of the men asked the question of all questions: "It says here that you've chosen domestic violence awareness as your platform. Can you tell us why?"

The questionnaire I had filled out and submitted prior to competition day had asked which platform I would advocate for if I was victorious in the pageant. When I had prepared the form, choosing DV Awareness was easy given my history with the issue. In my head, I knew I wanted to somehow help women like my mother and myself, but I hadn't worked out the details of what that would look like yet.

"Well…" I could feel my eyes welling up with emotion. I urged myself to stay composed as I dropped my head, ashamed of what I was about to say.

As much as I wanted to, I couldn't look them in the eye. "As I mentioned earlier, I am from the island of Trinidad and my mother went through it with my father there. My siblings and I grew up witnessing really brutal stuff. Machetes and beer bottles used against her in the name of what our father called love and discipline, and well, you see..."

The tears were warm and plentiful as they burst out of my eyes and streamed down my made-up cheeks. It had been ten years since I last had to publicly recount the abuse in a courtroom full of strangers, and now here I was, once again believing I would be negatively judged based on my choosing to stay in a relationship like that.

"Do you need to take a break, Ms. Anderson?" one of the women said as she reached over with a tissue. I saw the white of it in the corner of my eye and lifted my head slightly so I could see to receive it.

"No, I'm okay, but I deeply apologize for being overcome with emotion. I hadn't envisioned the interview going this way. This issue runs deep for me and... Again, I apologize," I said tearfully as I wiped my wet face.

"You don't have to apologize. Take your time and continue when you're ready."

With a few deep breaths, I somewhat composed myself and continued. "Thank you very much. Well, you see, I grew up saying I would never be the person receiving the kind of love our father dished out to her. I always said I would do better. My mother was financially dependent on him and barely had an education, and I wanted to be different. While I did go on to receive an education and become an independent professional, none of that made a difference since I, too, ended up in an abusive relationship at the age of 21 that lasted for almost two years. The last time he beat on me, it lasted from about 9:00 the night before till about 2:00 the next morning. I decided to go to the hospital for the first time after that attack, to seek help for the injuries I had sustained. It made him really upset when I told him I was breaking things off, and he then tried to break into my apartment after I had the locks changed. I finally called the police, but then he started stalking me, so I got a restraining order. He adhered to that and thankfully hasn't bothered me since. It took some time, but I realized that none of it was my fault, nor was anything my mother endured her fault. I now want to help others understand that this can happen to anyone by sharing my story."

Once I was through, I felt like the long explanation was more of a ramble. My head still slumped in shame, I continued soaking the tissue that was now brown from my makeup. I willed my head to rise so my eyes could reconnect with the panel. The male judge who had originally asked the unknowingly loaded question still lacked readable emotion. Because of that, I just knew I had ruined my chances of being a viable competitor. They had probably written me off as a weak, down-trodden cry baby when they were looking for a pleasant, assertive, strong woman to wear their crown. None of the pageant competitors I had seen on TV ever seemed to have a checkered past like mine. What the hell was I doing here?

As I finished drying my face and regained my composure, one of the female judges spoke. "That was really brave of you, Ms. Anderson. You and your mom survived something that you never asked to be put through." This comment made me lift my head all the way, and when I did, I saw that both female panel members were wiping tears away, too.

"That's all the questions we have for you, so why don't you take a moment to regroup over there before you exit the room. I think we have everything we need here, right?" she asked the rest of the group. They all nodded in agreement.

I thanked them for their time, stood up, and walked over to the right of the room where the judge had directed me to head. Back turned to the panel, I took a few long, deep breaths. After a few seconds I felt a light tap on my shoulder. I turned to see that it was the other female judge, and she was smiling at me.

"Thank you, young lady, for being transparent about what happened to you and your mom. I know firsthand that it took a lot of courage. I was also in a situation years ago that I am glad I left. I'm glad you and your mom survived."

Wait a minute! This beautiful woman, this embodiment of class and grace standing before me, was saying she too had been involved in an abusive relationship? I was so taken aback, I wasn't sure how to respond. My entire perception of the demographic this issue affected had been dismantled in an instant.

"Thank you very much."

"Whatever happened to your father?" She asked.

"He died in Trinidad in a hospital room, alone, from natural causes at 50 years old."

"Well if that ain't *karma*, I don't know what is. What about your mom?"

"She is well and thriving these days, thank God, and works as a CNA at a hospital," I shared proudly.

"Oh praise God, I am glad to hear that! Well, you keep being a light for others and sharing from your heart as you did today, and never, ever apologize for your truth," she said firmly.

"Thank you. I won't." I took one last deep breath as she walked away from me and made my way to the exit door.

"Thank you all for your time. Have a good rest of the day," I said as I exited. After I closed the door behind me, I stood outside the room for a couple of minutes soaking up the judge's last words to me. I couldn't get over the fact that she had once been a victim, too. I was also overwhelmed that she believed my platform was going to be worth my effort. It was the first time I had shared what happened to me for a positive event, and I didn't care now what it meant for my scores in the competition. At that moment, it felt like I had already won because I had taken a little bit more of my power back.

I arrived back in the dressing room where all the other contestants waited. Some were getting ready for the next round of the competition in a frenzy, while others were waiting to complete the interview round I had just come from.

"Sooooo, how'd it go?" one of the girls asked.

"I honestly don't know, but I'm glad it's over. Good luck in there!" I said as I rejoined the excited group getting ready for the next round.

The moment to step onto the stage in our first outfit of the evening came, and the butterflies in my stomach were back. When my name was called, I don't think I had ever channeled my mother more. Her effortless style and grace were all I thought about in that moment, walking out to bright lights and the dark sea of a loudly cheering audience. Mummy, my best friend, and other invited guests were in attendance that night, and even though I

*Evening Gown part
of the pageant*

couldn't see them, I distinctly heard their cries of support in the crowd. After the first few steps onto the stage, it felt like I was gliding on air. I was eager to show the judges grace, despite the sorrow they saw from me earlier. I hoped my personality would shine through.

Throughout the rest of the competition, I switched from a state of anxious hair and wardrobe changes to a sense of calm walking each time I stepped onto the stage. The on-stage calm stayed with me through the evening gown portion and a question from the judges. The advice from pageant team members the night before was to take it slow and enjoy, and I had zero problem doing that. I was ready to be done with this dare and tell my friends, "There! Y'all satisfied? I did it and I did not fall not one time on that stage!"

With all parts of the competition complete, I stood with the other contestants as we waited on stage for the results to be tallied up. I had to use the bathroom and felt a little hungry, but kept my poise.

With the results being delivered, it dawned on me that the third and second runner-ups had been announced, and there were only two of us left. Then, they announced the first runner-up's name. It wasn't mine.

"And the winner of this year's inaugural Ethnic New England pageant is Ms. Lovern Anderson! Congratulations!" The announcer's voice boomed and the crowd exploded in applause. *Wait a minute! Whaaaatttt? Me?* I was completely stunned.

"You won!" said the first runner up as she hugged me. The other contestants joined in for an excited group hug. I was overwhelmed, surprised, and thrilled all at once.

"Now you go out to L.A. to represent Boston fiercely in the nationals!" the first runner-up told me over the victory music.

*Receiving hug from 1st Runner-up and being
crowned by pageant director, Janelle*

"I'm sorry, what? L.A.? Oh no, no, no... See, I didn't think I would win anything so I can't go to L.A.! You can take my place! Yeah, you can take my place! There you go!" *That's a perfect plan,* I thought, wanting to share my joy with her.

"Uh, no, honey, that's not how this works. You are going! You will do amazing and bring back that crown!"

I was whisked away for the crowning and the traditional first walk as the new Ethnic New England Queen. My family and friends greeted me at the foot of the stage with congratulations, flowers, and hugs. I had just won a freaking beauty pageant! A surreal turn of events on this journey to say the least, but it's truly a night I will never, ever forget. Needless to say, during the next girls night dinner, my friends all good-naturedly had to eat their words of doubt and never dared this girl again.

***

Leading up to September that year, I prepped for the national leg of competition in Los Angeles, California. My competitive edge had now kicked in and I wanted to win, so I put in a little more effort into preparation this time around. On the day of competition, I noticed right away that it was on a completely different level than the local leg. The women were from all different states, each the winner of their own local pageant, and they had all brought their game faces. Meeting the other contestants came with an unexpectedly high

Night of pageant National Competition and 2nd win – Los Angeles, California

level of intimidation that made me uneasy. Not because anyone was mean to me, but because I had started to psych myself out. It took a little bit of time to snap out of that mindset.

Competition day came around, and my nerves were incredibly high again. I went through the various rounds that evening, again channeling my mother's grace, and managed to have some fun with it. She and the Boston squad couldn't make it to L.A., but some of my local family members were in the audience to support me. They cheered and showed me amazing support every time I stepped on stage, which really helped me feel more at ease.

The majority of that evening was a blur. Before I knew it, all of the contestants from my division were lined up awaiting our results. Once again, it came down to me and one other beautiful woman left on the stage after all the runner-ups had been named. I said a little prayer in my head before the winner was announced: *This time I am prayerful I win Lord, 'cause you didn't bring me this far to not let me walk away with the crown, right? If this is your will, let it be done.*

"And this year's Ethnic World International winner is... Lovern Anderson! Congratulations to you!"

With even more people in attendance at this national event, the crowd reaction to my win was deafening. I was much more calm about the news of winning this time around as congratulatory hugs came from the other fellow contestants, but boy did I thank God profusely in that moment. My mind was already back home, thinking about how I could now use this new voice to help others. Now I had two pageant titles with one year to put in the work and make a difference. I was ready. God had just told me so.

CHAPTER 19:
The Year of Advocacy and Glam

I returned to Boston with the second title win in hand. It all felt dream-like and I was soaking up everything that came with it. Photoshoots and professional hair and makeup jobs were definitely not the norm for me, but it felt good to look and feel fabulous!

My colleagues at work loved that I had done so well during the competition. One afternoon as we headed to a networking event together, my boss shared how proud she was of my accomplishment and choice of platform. I took the opportunity to open up and share a little with her about why I was so passionate about domestic violence awareness. As she listened, her face betrayed her shock at what I had to say. I told her about the random attacks I endured during lunch breaks at our old office location, the harassing phone calls I received at my desk, being homeless for a couple weeks and doing what I had to do to show up to work seeming and looking as normal as possible. I also told her how I'd always felt I dare not disclose any of this for fear of being fired for bringing drama to work or being stereotyped as the black woman with ghetto issues.

Her response was surprisingly empathetic. She stated she had no idea any of that was happening to me when I worked for her prior. She said she absolutely would have helped me seek help if I had disclosed the abuse

Various Photoshoots as the Ethnic World International Titleholder

to her. Then, she shared a little bit about a domestic violence situation her friend had experienced, and commended me for moving forward with my plan of advocacy. The exchange brought us both to tears. Our conversation was cut short as we pulled up to our scheduled event, but upon exiting her car, she hugged me in support. Her reiteration that I was a valued employee who would not have been fired then for what was being done to me, and that she valued me as a person beyond the color of my skin, was invaluable and something I carry with me still today.

Over the next few days, I began to think about which direction I wanted to go in with a DV Awareness campaign. It dawned on me that I had never heard about help for women and girls experiencing abuse in the community I lived in, which primarily consisted of people of color. To my recollection, the local health center I frequented never had fliers up about it. I also didn't remember the issue highlighted frequently on news programs or commercials I had seen over the years. There seemed to be nothing, so I would need to start from the ground up.

I started attending various networking events where I shared my experience as a domestic violence survivor. I had read somewhere in my research that one in every four women would experience abuse in their lifetime, so that could be anyone in a group of four women I was chatting with at these events. These women probably thought, just like me, that they were the only ones in their circle who had gone through it. I needed to help them debunk that myth.

Sharing my experiences one-on-one or in small groups at these events was not easy. I forced myself to push through the discomfort of talking about the issue with so many strangers after I realized that anyone, even the beautiful judge from the pageant panel, could fall prey to abuse. So many times, the conversations went really well around the traditional networking chit-chat where people asked what I did for a living. I responded with my day job details, but also included the platform I was advocating for and why. This part usually garnered me solemn stares in return, and then the people I was talking to would find a way to wrap up the conversation or find someone else to turn around and chat with. However, there was something else that never failed to happen at these events. At least one or

CBS Local – Centro program

WHDH's – Urban
Update program

Radio appearances representing the pageant to raise awareness around DV

two women would share that they, too, had been involved in an abusive situation or knew someone who had gone through it. They always thanked me for helping others to understand the issue from a survivor's standpoint. When this happened, it made all the uncomfortable interactions worth it.

Some of those conversations eventually led me to some guest appearances on TV and radio programs centered on my community. I was able to share pieces of my story that I knew would resonate with any woman watching, regardless of race. I wanted to let them know that any shame related to what they had felt was not theirs to carry, and that there was life after leaving or escaping abuse. The appearances were amazing, but it still was not enough.

Around this time, one of the connections I met in passing introduced me to a vibrant soul who was just as energized about awareness as I was. I was surprised to find out that this person was a he, and his day job was hosting batterer intervention meetings. This was refreshing coming from a man. I loved his whole vibe immediately. His name was Antonio, and he would not only become a dear friend, but also a long-time colleague in this work.

Antonio shared information with me about the statewide White Ribbon Day (WRD) campaign, which asks men and boys to speak out against domestic violence and become allies in the fight to eradicate the issue. I thought the idea of WRD was brilliant! After all, women are not the main perpetrators of DV, so involving men and boys to talk to other men and boys about ways they could be part of the solution was necessary. I had never heard of anything like this in my community, so I decided to organize one.

After Anthony introduced me to a local WRD campaign coordinator, I decided to stage my event at a public library. Male WRD

Antonio listening in on remarks of the Community WRD

representatives attended and shared reasons why it is important to have men and boys become part of the conversation. They also led participants in taking the White Ribbon Day Pledge, which in part asks people to never condone violence against any girl or woman. I invited friends and while only about 20 people showed up, it was 20 more than yesterday who now knew about the issue at hand.

Mummy listening in during my remarks at Walk-A-Thon

With the WRD event completed, I still felt I could do more to spread the word. I thought about all the awareness walks I had heard about or attended over the years, and didn't think any of them had centered around domestic violence. I decided to organize a Walk-A-Thon that summer that would benefit a local DV agency.

I contacted the agency to find out about services they offered, and was blown away to find out how much they did to help victims and survivors. They had services like emergency shelter, group and individual counseling, legal advocacy, safety planning, and more. This disbanded the dreary myth I had believed for so very long about shelters and what they do.

Organizing the Walk-A-Thon was a lot of work, but incredibly worth it in the end. The event highlighted the local agency's work and gave community members a chance to publicly state that abuse was wrong. My friends and family volunteered, my pageant sisters attended in support, as complete strangers even showed up after hearing about the walk through social media or word-of-mouth. The turnout was another affirmation that my community had an appetite for more education on the issue of domestic violence. The absolute highlight was having Mummy beside me that day. I couldn't help but get emotional as she stood next to me at the culmination of the walk. Nothing could top that.

The success of the Walk-A-Thon got me fired up to do even more on the awareness front. As the summer progressed, I wanted to see firsthand what an emergency abuse shelter was like. I had been advocating for people to seek help, but needed to know what help really looked like. I had no idea whether the image that flashed in my head all those years ago, while sitting in the emergency room seeking treatment for my injuries, was an accurate depiction. I connected with the agency the Walk-A-Thon had benefited to find out how I could volunteer at their shelter. They had an opening for a weekend volunteer to play with the kids housed at the shelter to give their mothers some alone time. I love kids, so this would be a win-win for me.

I was told that in order to enter the shelter space, they would have a background check performed and I would have to take part in a DV-101 Training, which would certify me as a Domestic Violence Advocate. The background check seemed like business as usual, but a training? I was always open to learning, but didn't think there was anything about abuse I could be taught after living it myself.

I started the training early that September with a small group of classmates. The class was led by a few agency representatives, including the shelter's director. Less than an hour into training, my mind was already blown by the facts presented. They taught us about the root causes of domestic violence, different types of abuse, how many people are affected by domestic violence, how to support victims seeking to leave their situation, bystander intervention, and so much more.

By the training's completion, my eyes were fully opened to the epidemic at hand and how much DV agencies did to help eradicate it. Before departing that day, I pulled the shelter director aside and asked her if there was anything they needed that I could help with, in addition to sitting with the kids. She explained the residents, many of whom arrived with just the clothes on their backs, received a new sheet set and pillow when they entered the shelter. "We typically run low on the bed linen and if anything, we could always use more of that."

"Say no more!" I responded excitedly. I was ready to help replenish the shortage they had with a bedding drive. I had also learned during the training that October is Domestic Violence Awareness Month. What better way to heighten awareness than to host this drive in September and October? I began to spread the word to my network about the bedding drive with word-of-mouth and social media, and posted flyers about it at businesses I frequented.

I also began volunteering at the shelter. The day I started, I was given directions to the safely guarded location and a tour of the house. Prior to this, I had been under the impression that victims were housed in a big open building filled with twin beds, similar to the homeless shelters I had seen on TV shows. Instead, I walked into a house that had a spacious eat-in kitchen, living room, dining room, play space for the children, laundry area, and an enclosed back yard. Each resident occupied their own bedroom and shared the bathrooms. The shelter staff also had a dedicated office space on the property. This was not at all what I had envisioned; I was pleasantly surprised, to say the least!

A staff member gave me the rundown of how many kids were there that day as she showed me the play space. I took a seat on a child-sized chair and watched the kids mill about. Their ages ranged from toddlers to seven or eight years old. While an enthusiastic group of younger kids immediately started playing with me, the older ones were reluctant to join in and seemed hesitant about my presence. It took a couple more weekends for them to warm up to me. One day, I asked one of the older girls if she would make me something from the jewelry kit she was playing with. She happily agreed and that was the opening for her and I to become friends. This exchange encouraged the other wonderful older children to warm up to me as well. I still have the bracelet she made me.

As with some of the kids in the beginning, a couple of the women housed at the shelter who didn't have children were hesitant about my presence.

I had my first conversation with one of them after several weeks of volunteering. The tall, sturdy Latina woman came into the playspace and sat down on the opposite side of the child-sized table where toys were scattered about. After greeting me, she asked my name and how I liked playing with the kids every weekend. I gushed about how much I loved it. She asked what brought me there to volunteer, and I shared that I, too, was a survivor. I explained a little about my story and some of my mother's. She initially refused to believe me because "no man would put his hands on a girl like you." That stuck with me because she was just like me in the beginning, when I believed that DV only affected a certain type of person. Before I knew about how wide the demographics really were, I certainly would never have walked by this woman on the street and thought she was a survivor, either.

When I was through telling her my story, she shared that she was a lesbian survivor and the last brutal attack by her partner involved her head being smashed into a glass table. That attack had landed her in the ER and then at the shelter where she and I were now talking. She pointed out the stitched-up area on the side of her head, visible under her low haircut. She nonchalantly stated that she had called it quits with her partner and was ready to move on with her life. I listened in horror to her ordeal, scared for her safety but appeased that she realized she needed to stay away from her attacker. As we chatted, I shared with her that I was inspired by her resiliency and proud of her progress.

That same afternoon as I was getting ready to leave, another reluctant resident approached me in the living room area and asked how I was doing. She looked to be in her early fifties, slender and Caucasian, with short red hair. After I answered her question, she told me that she thought it was nice that I spent time with the kids. She shared that she had kids of her own who were grown and off doing big things in the world. She alluded to the fact that she had once lived a posh life, but suffered financial and emotional abuse at the hands of her ex-husband that left her destitute. She had hidden her troubles from her children for years, not wanting them to know how bad it had become.

The following weekend, I met a resident who was eight months pregnant. She was tall, slender, African American, and looked to be in her mid-twenties. She looked no more than four months pregnant from the size of her stomach. I later learned that her boyfriend had kicked her down a flight of stairs during her last attack. She had suffered so much stress during the pregnancy, it resulted in her carrying very small.

My time at the shelter showed me there is no barrier as to who is affected by domestic violence; anyone, of any age, of any race, coming from any economic background, can find themselves the victim of abuse. This fact was something I had learned during the advocacy training, but as a volunteer, I got to see it up close and personal.

Over the next month, I did my best to have a successful bedding drive for the wellbeing of the women and children. I put myself in their shoes. What if I had accepted the help the ER doctor had offered me back then, and ended up in a shelter? I would definitely have loved a new sheet and pillow set. It would have helped me feel human, and given me something of my own. To be able to lie down on a clean bed, in a safe space the morning after I left the hospital would have meant the world.

With that in mind, I set up shop once again at the beautiful local library where I had hosted the WRD event, because I knew so many people frequented the space on the weekends. I was able to meet new folks and connect with some familiar friends one-on-one about the drive and awareness overall, letting everyone know I would be back the following weekend if they decided they wanted to donate new linen. Additionally, I handed out flyers about the drive to people in cars on a busy street while they were stopped in traffic, enlightening them about why their donation was so important. I asked them to come by the following weekend to drop off their donation of a new twin sheet or a pillow, since I would be set up on that street again to collect them. Some folks drove forward as if I were about to deliver the plague when I approached their cars, but that only doubled my enthusiasm to talk to the next carload who might want to listen about how they could help.

The drive was a total success because folks did come back the following weekend with their donations! The amount of gratitude I had for every single person that was moved to donate was insurmountable. Someone was going to rest easier because of their generosity, and that was priceless!

Street-side set-up to collect linen from driver-bys

Library patrons donating to the Bedding Drive

Appearance at event honoring then-Massachusetts Governor, Deval Patrick

All of these initiatives coupled with my day job, scheduled appearances as a pageant title holder, speaking engagements, and spending time at home, made my life hectic to say the least. Even so, I wanted to spread even more awareness.

That winter, I saw an advertisement from the American Red Cross stating that they were looking for people to donate blood for patients with blood loss from traumatic injuries. I had never donated because I was not a fan of needles, but I felt driven to do so after seeing the compelling ad. It made me think of victims of domestic violence rushed to ER and needing blood

Awareness presentation for girls group

after an attack that resulted in blood loss. I put my fear of needles aside and found a local drive to give a pint of my red stuff, knowing my donation would help save three lives in need.

Around the same time of the blood drive, a colleague of mine, Brent, told me about an upcoming five-mile race in honor of fallen first responders. This piqued my interest. During the agency's training, I had learned that DV calls are some of the most lethal for first responders and wanted to do the run in honor of those lost to this issue. The run was set for the following May, during the Memorial Day Weekend, so I agreed to train and participate in the race with Brent. My other coworkers thought I would give up because I was not a fan of running in the chilly weather, but by now we all know what happens when Lovern is issued a challenge.

Brent and I started eating at our desks and using our lunch breaks to run for about twenty minutes each day, then shower quickly and get back to our desk in time to start working again. Some days we opted to speed walk, other days we would slowly jog, but almost everyday during the week, we moved to keep those muscles loose. When it got closer to the day of the

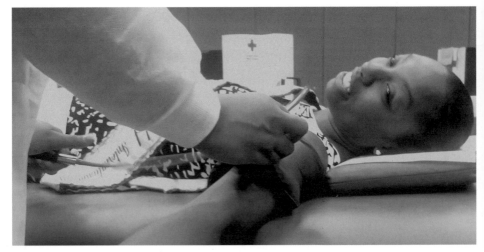

First blood drive donation

race, we met on weekends to run farther and longer than we could during the work day.

Sunday of the Memorial Day weekend finally arrived, the morning sunny and a little chilly. Hundreds of people had converged at the Boston Seaport's World Trade Center for the event. It was exciting to see up close. After the race's opening ceremony concluded, Brent and I lined up behind the starting point with the other participants. The "go" signal was given, and we were off! The throngs of spectators and loud music felt exhilarating at first, but by a mile in, I was winded. Between the hilly landscape (which we had not trained on prior), the brisk air that morning, and being overwhelmed by the crowd of runners around me, I just needed to stop running and walk to catch my breath. Brent was supportive and walked with me. I felt better after a few minutes and we picked up the pace again. The run took us through historical and beautiful areas of Downtown Boston, and as the morning progressed and the sun rose higher in the sky, I marveled at the city's beauty.

As we neared the finish line, we could hear cheers of onlookers as they encouraged everyone to push through to the end. My name and finishing time were announced over the loudspeaker as I crossed the finish line. What a rush! The race had taken me a little over an hour to complete and I was elated to have completed it in remembrance of those who lost their lives while seeking to protect victims.

Lovern and Brent at their first 5 mile for Boston's Run To Remember

With the race under my belt, I rested up that summer and flew back to Los Angeles in September for the 2012 Ethnic World International finals. Crowning my successor was bittersweet because I had truly enjoyed my year of unexpected glam and advocacy that would now always be a part of me.

You feel proud of yourself. You feel stronger now. You feel less anxious, and you thank yourself for validating your own feelings — for owning your story. For trusting your gut. For claiming your right to healthy relationships.

*Source: OneLove https://www.joinonelove.org/learn/
what-it-was-like-to-start-dating-again-after-my-unhealthy-relationship/*

*Backstage at the 2012 Ethnic
World International Finals*

*Post successor crowning
at end of the night*

Lovern's Self-Care Suggestions:

- Stretching
- Set boundaries
- Seek counseling
- Write in a journal
- Get enough sleep
- Allow yourself to cry
- Praying (favorite of mine)

- Do things that bring you joy
- Make time away from phone
- Read inspirational literature/ quotes daily
- Stay in contact with important people in your life

I needed to learn how to love myself, spend time with myself, appreciate myself, all before I could be open to healthy love from someone else. All of the above suggestions helped me get to the core of what I needed to do just that. Self-care was not selfish of me. It was and continues to be self preservation.

CHAPTER 20:
Healthy Love Comes When
You Least Expect It

As they say, all work and no play makes Jane a dull pageant title holder. Around the same time that I was prepping for the national leg of the competition, a friend of mine thought I had been working way too much and needed some fun in my life. Unbeknownst to me, she set up a profile of me on the infamous match.com dating website. I was mortified when she told me what she had done, but she soon had me convinced that there was no harm in seeing who was out there. The more I thought about it, she was right. Why not?

Growing up in the Caribbean, it was understood that a decent girl would grow up to find a "good man" who would marry her, and they would go on to have kids together. With my father being as strict as he was, teen dating had been frowned upon. When I started seeing someone just before I left the island the first time, we saw each other in secret so Lloydie would not think I was going against his rules.

The definition of dating means to actively get out there and meet people, spend time with them, and decide whether you like their mannerisms and habits. It means you're on a search to find a suitable partner to enter into a relationship with. In my culture, however, once you are at a suitable age, the first "good" man you end up with is the man you are supposed to marry. Otherwise you're looked upon as improper or a slut for flitting from man to man without making a commitment.

I was a big girl now and decided I would give this dating thing a try. After the profile was set up, I began to get email alerts from the site. There were about five suitors that landed in my inbox and it felt liberating to sift through their profiles, picking and choosing who I wanted to exchange messages with first. I was like a kid in a candy store.

That summer, I actually dated! Casual, always public meet-ups for a bite or a scenic walk. The men were from all different ethnicities, including my own, and while it was fun, I always ultimately found something wrong with them by the end of the first date. Very few made it to a second date.

One afternoon late that summer, I was dropping something off for my friend Janelle, who was also my pageant director. Her then-fiance, Hansley, and his friend were playing basketball outside as I arrived. Just before I left, she mentioned there was someone she thought I should meet because she thought he would be a good fit for me to go out with. It turned out to be Carson, her fiance's friend who I had passed by on the way in.

"Awwww, heck no! I am all set," I responded hastily.

"Why though? He's a good man," she replied.

"So are all the other men I've been dating. All set," I said sarcastically.

"But he's financially stable, too!" she fired back.

"So are all these other guys I've been seeing," I said, standing firm.

"Look, he's single and Jamaican."

"Oh well, that really doesn't do anything to help his case, so right about now, I'm gonna make my exit! Okay, bye!" I rushed out the door, barely waving goodbye to the men as they played their one-on-one game under the summer sun.

I wasn't totally unfamiliar with the guy Janelle wanted to set me up with. He and I were friends on Facebook because of our mutual friends. I was set to do a poetry reading for Hansley's and Janelle's wedding later that fall and he was going to be a groomsman, so naturally we had connected on social media. Outside of what I saw online, I didn't know much about Carson. He seemed harmless and unassuming, but I had preconceived notions about Jamaican men after being around a fair amount of not-so-good ones in the past. In my head, they were all grouped together as philandering, impolite, and ego-driven. I had no time to be around anyone with that type of energy, so I was sure I wouldn't even entertain the thought of dating him.

In Mid-September I flew to Los Angeles with Janelle for the national competition, alongside another pageant sister who was going to compete in a different division. As we all headed to the hotel in a cab from the airport, Janelle and I realized we had received a group Facebook message from Carson. I began to read his message aloud to the girls from the back seat of the cab: "Hello Janelle and Lovern, I just wanted to take the time to congratulate you guys on a job well done. The Ethnic New England Pageant should be very proud of your appearance on the Channel 7 - Urban Update show. They couldn't have asked for better representation. You both looked and sounded professional and I'm honored to tell people you are my friends. You guys are superstars in the making and more TV is definitely in your future. Keep up the good work ladies. (Good luck in L.A., Lovern!)"

Hmmm, impressive and sweet, I thought as I read. Then, the message abruptly took on a hilarious tone where he made fun of himself and made us all erupt in laughter.

"He is a funny one!" I said mid-laugh, the girls nodding and laughing in agreement. As the giggles died down, I blurted out, "Maybe I should just ask him to be my date to your wedding."

"Who's him?" Janelle asked inquisitively.

"Carson," I said nonchalantly.

"Wait, what? Really?" Janelle asked in surprise.

"Well, yeah. I mean, we'll both be in the wedding, so why not?"

"Yes! Why not! Oh, I am super excited about this!" Janelle responded excitedly while my other pageant sister clapped in agreement.

"Okay great, but don't get too excited, guys. It just makes sense to go with him. I'll reply to his message separately to ask him to reach out."

As we continued to the hotel in the cab, I took a couple minutes to send a response. I thanked Carson for his well wishes and asked him to be my date for the event, providing my phone number for us to chat further. That was Saturday afternoon.

Why the sudden change of heart around the man I had previously wanted nothing to do with? Even though the dating scene was going well for me, I realized that I wasn't prepared to attend the wedding of two close friends with anyone I was casually dating. I wasn't a fan of Jamaican men, but I was tickled pink by Carson's eloquent message and saw no harm in attending this public event together.

The incredibly busy weekend of nationals flew by so quickly, ending with me winning the pageant. I announced my win on Facebook at the end of the night, and my timeline was immediately flooded with well wishes from friends and family.

That Monday, it really began to set in that I had indeed won my division. All the well wishes on my timeline were answered, but I still had some inbox messages to respond to. Once I was done, it dawned on me that Carson hadn't responded to my ask even though it had been two days. Was he ignoring me or blowing me off? I relayed my reservation about his lack of response to the girls, and they also thought it was strange.

We left L.A. the next morning to fly back to Massachusetts, happy with the success of the trip and glad to be going home. After we all left the airport in Boston to head our separate ways, I had a few more messages in my inbox including one from Carson. The message had come in while I was mid-flight. In it, he congratulated me on the win and provided his home and cell phone numbers, stating he would be honored to be my date. He concluded by saying he was looking forward to chatting with me. While his message was nice, I was put off that he took that long to reply. I decided I would make him wait for that chat, just like he had made me wait for his "yes."

After I settled into bed around 9:00 pm that Thursday night, I finally called him on the house number he had provided. He answered on the second ring.

"Hi, it's Lovern," I said in a relaxed tone.

"Oh, hey! How's it going?" Carson asked.

"Great. I'm looking forward to the wedding and glad you are, as you say, 'honored' to be my date," I said coyly.

"Oh, you are huh?" He matched my tone with his response.

"Yeah, yeah, I am, but tell me, why exactly did it take you so long to respond to my ask? Did you have an inbox full of women asking you out on dates last weekend that you needed to get to sift through?" I asked sarcastically. I was still riding the high of dating lots of eligible men over the last few months. It had lifted my confidence quite a bit, to the point where his lack of response had profoundly perplexed me. I couldn't help but bring it up. My derisive questions made him laugh out loud.

"Oh, I am so glad I amused you there," I said. I needed to let him know how peeved I still was.

"You are funny," he said, coming down from his laughter. "Actually, I just got caught up doing some work for a neighbor of mine, and didn't get a chance to respond until Tuesday. I apologize if I offended you."

"So it was unexpected work on a weekend that kept you from typing 'yes, I'll go with you', huh? What exactly do you do that allows you to help your neighbor all weekend?" I said, again flexing my sarcasm muscles.

"Well, I'm a licensed electrician and this was a side job that needed to be wrapped up in order to help her have light going forward, so actually, yeah, it did take much of my weekend, unfortunately. I'm also studying for the Master Electrician exam and took some time to study for it Sunday evening and Monday once the job wrapped up." As he summarized his weekend, I noticed his Jamaican accent was very prevalent. I felt a little bad for being ready to hang him out to dry after he gave this reasonable explanation.

"Okay, well I guess you can be forgiven if that's the case," I responded sweetly.

"Forgiven? Guess you had me on the bad list all this time, huh? Hope you don't think I was blowing you off?"

"Oh no, not at all. I was just messing with ya." I hoped my response was believable.

"Okay, good. Oh, and congrats again on the win. That must have been exciting."

"Thank you very much! It was. I am proud, but glad it's over. I can honestly say now that I tip my hat to women who take part in pageants. It's not just dresses, heels, and makeup; there's a lot of work involved. I am really excited to work on my platform of domestic violence awareness, too."

"Oh yeah? What made you pick that subject?" he asked.

I had avoided this question from anyone I dated since I didn't even tell most of the guys I was involved in pageants. Since Carson had been following my pageant journey on social media already, it felt okay to share the basics of why I'd chosen DV as my platform. After divulging a little about being a child witness in Trinidad and a little about the adult relationship that made me a survivor in the States, Carson shared his belief that abuse against women was abhorrent. He told me a little about his life growing up in Jamaica before migrating to the States in the late eighties, admitting in the process that he had never known anyone who had experienced domestic violence.

The conversation shifted and we started reminiscing about growing up Caribbean, sharing common experiences about childhood that made us both laugh. We shared fond memories of attending high school in the States, information about our current careers, and shared interests in movies, music, and signing artists.

My cell phone then suddenly gave a beep alert.

"Hold on a minute, my phone's beeping." I took the phone off my ear to look at it, and it showed that I had 5% battery life left. What's more, the time was after 2:00 in the morning! "Oh my entire word, do you know what time it is?" I asked.

"Oh wow, I can't believe it's that late!" Carson responded in amazement.

"I know, right? I guess you talk too much, sir."

"Oh, you can't pin that solely on me, miss," he said with a laugh.

"Alright, it was both of us. I really enjoyed talking with you, so I guess it's true what they say: time flies…"

"When you're having fun," we both finished in unison.

"Yes, yes, that, but I have to grab some z's. You can give me a ring later today after work if you want." I said.

"Sure. Well, enjoy your sleep. I enjoyed your company too," he said.

I felt invigorated after we hung up. It was the most stimulating and effortless conversation I'd had in a while. Not that talking with other dates hadn't been good, but there was something safe and endearing, even comfortable, with Carson. I woke up the next day with a broad smile that lasted all the way through my commute. Over the next couple weeks, we continued to talk on the phone almost every night. I looked forward to our conversations and had stopped checking my match.com inbox.

The week of my 33rd birthday, I went on numerous dinner dates with girlfriends who wanted to celebrate my win from the pageant in conjunction with my special day. Carson and I were talking on the phone after one of those dinners when I mentioned that we had been talking all this time, but had barely discussed plans for our mutual friends' wedding.

"Well, why don't I finally take you out to dinner to celebrate your birthday, and we'll talk about it then?" he asked.

"Okay, yeah, sure. I mean, it would be weird that we hadn't met up in person before then, right? Might be really awkward?" This made us both chuckle.

"Yeah, just a little. So, it's settled. I'm taking you out so we aren't the awkward pair at the wedding. You pick a place you like and let me know." He was growing on me.

The next weekend we met at my favorite Asian restaurant, Buddachen. Leading up that night, I kept praying to myself: *Please Lord, let the chemistry flow over from the phone to in person! Even more importantly, please don't let me find anything wrong that makes me wanna quit him!*

The restaurant was closer to his apartment, so the night of our meet-up, I drove to him and parked my car outside his building so we could carpool. As I walked over to his car, he stood at the passenger side waiting to let me in with a big, welcoming smile on his face. He looked different from the times I had seen him in passing. As I walked closer, I noticed that his well-groomed dreadlocks were long enough to rest on his chest on top of his hip-length leather jacket.

"Hey you!" I said when I got closer.

"Hey yourself. You look nice," he said as he opened the car door, giving me the once over.

"Why, thank you!" I responded.

We instinctively extended our arms outward for a quick embrace. He had long arms that encased all of me and he smelled like expensive cologne. We let go of each other and I stepped into the car, both of us making sure my clothing was out of the way as he closed the door. Using my *Bronx Tale* manners, I reached over to his side of the car and opened the door so he could get in.

"Well, there's a first! I never had a beautiful woman open my door for me before I got to it. Thanks," he said in surprise.

For the first time, I explained the scene from the movie as we drove to the restaurant and we shared a good laugh over it.

"So does this mean you *like me,* like me?" Carson asked, which made me giggle because I had given myself away with the explanation.

We pulled up to the restaurant, headed into the charming, mood-lit setting, and grabbed a corner table. It was his first time there, so he asked me for recommendations. When the waiter came, we ordered right away. As the waiter walked away, Carson made a joke about one of the dishes' names that made me laugh out loud. I covered my mouth so as not to disturb other patrons.

We talked for hours over delicious food, and he complimented my choice of venue. When dessert was served I finally checked the time and realized we had been in the restaurant for three hours! We decided to wrap up the night, so Carson settled the bill and we headed back to his car. I offered to drive back, and he accepted.

On the drive back, my stomach became flooded with butterflies as we sat at one of the stop lights between the restaurant and his place. I had really enjoyed the date, and thanked God the chemistry did indeed carry over in person. I really did *like him*, like him, but he seemed too good to be true. I was still searching for anything that might squash the potential for a second, third, or fourth date. We pulled off from that light and I knew we would meet the next one soon. *I'm gonna kiss him*, I thought. *That will determine that he's a horrible kisser or that he has bad breath and that'll be a good reason right there. Perfect!*

We pulled up to the next light.

"I really had a nice time tonight. Thank you for an amazing birthday dinner."

Before he had a chance to say anything, I leaned in with my eyes halfway closed to initiate a lip lock. He did the same in response. His breath was warm and smelled like mint. His soft lips tasted like the popular strawberry Chapstick flavor. Our tongues hungrily searched for each other. The kiss sent shockwaves down the back of my neck and all through my spine. We were oblivious to everything around us. Someone pulled up behind our car and gave a brief honk of their horn to let us know that the light had turned green, which caused us to abruptly break our lip lock.

"Got it, Mr. We're going, we're going," I said, which made us both laugh.

"That was really nice, and dare I say, it topped dinner," Carson said.

He was right. The kiss was great and though dinner was tasty, it was now a far cry from his delicious lips. I didn't want the night to end yet. I found myself wanting to know more about this Jamaican man who was quickly dispelling all of my prior notions about the culture.

"I don't think I want our night to end now. Let's go dancing!" I blurted out.

"Oh yeah? Well, I don't want it to end either. I'm down for dancing. There's probably not enough time to head downtown to try and find parking and still have enough time to enjoy the night, but there is a closer neighborhood club we could check out if you want."

"As long as there's good music, I'll be good. I trust your judgement." I said. *He probably has no rhythm*, I thought, *and that right there would be the deal breaker.* Things were going way too well. He was a great conversationalist, made me laugh, looked and smelled great, and was a great kisser. Dancing would be the ultimate test.

"Okay, cool," he said. "In that case, keep going straight at the next light instead of taking a left. That street will take us right to the club."

We drove for about five more minutes and pulled up to a Caribbean themed club with easily accessible parking. Upon entering, he led me through the semi-packed crowd to a spot toward the back of the room where we could hang out. Amidst the loud music, he asked in my ear if I wanted something to drink. I said I did, so he left and came back shortly with two full cups.

As he set our drinks down, a mellow Trindadian Soca song I loved came on. It prompted me to take his hand in mine and initiate our first dance. I stepped over and stood in front of him, my back facing him, our bodies touching. We swayed to the beat of the music. His arms encased my waist and I let myself get lost in the music. It may sound cliche, but by the third song that the DJ seamlessly segued through, it seemed like Carson and I were the only ones in the room. I turned around to face him, resting my arms around his neck. Our eyes connected and we leaned in, now swaying much slower as we enjoyed the passion of another kiss.

Darn it. Not only can he dance, but he can dance while kissing! I thought in delighted exasperation.

We danced into the wee hours of the morning, only sitting out for two of the DJ's sets. We decided to leave just before the club closed for the night to avoid a crowded exit. He held my hand as we crossed the street to get back to the car. I felt at ease and comfortable. The entire night was effortless.

First public date at our friend's wedding

We pulled up next to where my car was parked and shared one more passionate kiss that seemed to last forever, his hands gently holding the sides of my neck. When it came to an end, he walked me to my car where we agreed to connect later that day. He waited for me to drive off. I left feeling at ease and smitten.

The following weekend, Hansley and Janelle's wedding day finally arrived. Carson and I decided we would meet up at the reception after each of our respective roles were served as groomsman and poem reader. It was a bright and sunny Fall afternoon, perfect for the outdoor ceremony which went off without a hitch. Our now-married friends looked amazing, and love was definitely in the air. Once the ceremony was over and the reception to-do's concluded, Carson and I connected and enjoyed each other's company. Our connection was palpable to some of our mutual friends in attendance, and many let us know they were happy to see it.

After a successful first public night out, we continued to meet up for romantic picnics, movie outings, dinner dates, and beach walks. We hung around his and my friends at different events, where we all had a great time. It turned out he had a lot of Trinidadian friends that had gotten him acclimated with the culture over the years.

After we'd been dating for a few months, Carson asked me if I wanted to attend his sister's birthday dinner, where his family would be in attendance. This was a big deal because he was extremely close with his family. I knew taking that step meant I wasn't just some girl, and he wanted the important people in his life to get to know me.

Over time I watched how much his siblings looked up to him, how he treated his mother with respect, the way he connected with his nieces and nephews, the way his friends looked to him as someone they could always

CarLove Picnic Date

Couple that introduced us – Hansley & Janelle

count on, his attention to detail around his work, and his drive to further his career in obtaining his Master Electrical License, which he ended up passing with flying colors. All of this triggered positive intuition in me about his overall character.

His admiration and care for me was right up there with everything else, and it showed. We had the usual level of lust and flirting that you'd expect in a new relationship, but that was not at the forefront. Carson thought about me before I even thought about myself. He valued my opinions, included me in decisions, trusted me at my word, always made time for me, and was great at lifting my spirits. So, a year and half later while we laid in bed watching TV, when

CarLove Engagement Photo

CarLove Wedding – 2012

Mummy and I on my wedding day

he asked me to marry him, I happily accepted. As the saying goes, "When you know, you know," and we knew. Carson and Lovern, aka CarLove, were set to become one.

Our families cheered us on during the wedding planning process, as well as the day of our union, and their support meant the world. Having Mummy walk me down the aisle that day was another phenomenal full-circle moment after all we had been through.

As part of the passion work we do at Love Life Now Foundation (LLN), it is imperative that we not only share what red flags are in unhealthy relationships where power and control is at the helm, but we also show what the green lights are in healthy ones where equality is the center. Our domestic violence awareness

CarLove Honeymoon – Turks and Caicos

workshops encompass pieces of my story as a backdrop. The workshops seek to educate and engage others about the ways they can be part of the solution, even if they have never been privy to abuse.

CHAPTER 21:
PTSD While Loving Life Now

As 2011 ended, so did my year of advocacy as a pageant title holder. While the pageant experience was amazing, I had no desire to compete going forward. I did, however, want to continue my advocacy work around domestic violence. A few contacts I made during that year had suggested I start a nonprofit to further my message. It wasn't long before I started looking into how to start a nonprofit from scratch.

One of the few people I shared the idea with was my best friend, Debbie. She and I chatted on the phone daily during our hour-long commutes, and she knew me better than most people. A trusted confidant since 1993, Debbie and I met one morning during our high school Algebra class. When the teacher asked a question, we competed over who could answer first. Once the class was over, my interest was piqued as to who this other smarty pants was. I struck up a conversation with her as we made our way to the lunchroom, and she mentioned that she had just migrated from the Caribbean island of Barbados. We found commonality there, and over the next few weeks became friends fairly quickly. We hung out together a lot over the next few years, dressing alike most days and wearing our hair the same. Our classmates and teachers commonly referred to us as "Laverne and Shirley," a reference to the late

Voted 'Class Pals' – Debbie and I during our High School Senior Year - 1996

1970's sitcom centered around two best friends and roommates who also worked together.

Debbie and I lost touch after high school when she went on to college and I had to go back to Trinidad. Even though our lives went in different directions, our bond never dissipated. Once we reconnected, it was as if no time had passed at all.

One morning during our commute, I talked about wanting to start a nonprofit to further the advocacy work I had done as a pageant title holder. I asked Debbie if she thought it crazy to even think about taking on more work amidst everything else I had going on.

"V..." The initial was short for the 'Vern' part of my name and the nickname she had used for me since high school. "As hard as I have seen you pour yourself into everything you've done so far, I think you'd be great at it! I mean, you already have the blueprint for what you want to do with all the initiatives you started this year. Plus, you know I'd be there to help you."

"That's all the confirmation I needed, D! What would I call it, though? I'd like it to include the 'Love' part of my name, cause that's what it's all about, right? Good and bad love, but also why more people should know what help looks like, and if you do experience bad love, why getting help isn't scary, 'cause it was never your fault."

"I totally agree. I mean, I never knew you went through all that stuff with that knucklehead until you told me, but look at you now. You've always been fierce, and that piece of you shined so much this year for something really, really good," she said. Her support and love were tangible through the phone. "What about Love Life Now? That's what you're doing, and you're such a good example of that to others after all you've been through."

"D, that's it right there! Love Life Now. My God, that's it. I absolutely love it! That's brilliant, babe!" I continued singing her praises as we wrapped up our morning commute call, and went into work fired up about my new potential foundation.

Over the next week, the fire in me continued to burn bright as I sought a board of directors for the Love Life Now Foundation, aka LLN. Debbie agreed to be one of them, as well as Antonio, who had helped make the initial White Ribbon Community Day a reality. Cassandre, who had introduced me to Antonio, believed wholeheartedly in the work we were setting out to do and agreed to be on the board as well.

Cassandre helped me map out the heart logo I had my heart set on, positioned Antonio's hands into the shape of a heart, and photographed them to ultimately bring the logo idea to life. The idea behind the logo was to highlight the generous hearts of the people who gave their time, energy, and supplies, because they would always be at the root of the foundation's advocacy work. That included men's voices as well,which is why we used male hands for the heart. We chose the color purple because it has been the color of domestic violence awareness since 1978, when nearly 100,000 purple-clad advocates marched on the capitol in Washington DC in support of equal rights.

With the website and bank account set up, I spent the next couple of weeks filling out the paperwork for IRS approval of 501c3 status. This would certify Love Life Now as a tax-exempt, charitable organization. Many evenings on my long commute home, I would spend at least thirty minutes on the phone, on hold, waiting to talk with an IRS repre-

Hearts and hands bringing awareness against domestic violence via our initiatives...

LLN Logo and Tagline

sentative so I could ask questions about the application. I wanted to make sure I was dotting my i's and crossing my t's before submitting. I finally submitted the paperwork in November 2011, and then the waiting began.

While we waited for the IRS' decision, the awareness work continued. We wanted to take the community White Ribbon Day to the next level and raise more awareness with men about how they could use their voices to speak out against abuse. This was important to me as I never forgot how I felt when the men in my neighborhood stood about, doing nothing to help Mummy as Lloydie attacked her. Even though these neighbors cared about our mother's

Sharing a word with LLN Board Member, Debbie prior to start of WRNG

Antonio leads an interactive discussion with the men at the 2012 WRNG about why their voices are needed on the DV awareness front.

well being, they felt they had no say in what happened in another man's house. I needed to help change that narrative in my community.

We didn't have a lot of funding at this point, but I will be forever indebted to local organizations like North Easton Savings and Harvard Pilgrim Healthcare, with whom I already had connections. As the saying goes, "your network is your net-worth," and I leaned into that as we began our initiatives to help get the foundation off the ground. We combined these investments with some of my own savings to launch our first White Ribbon Night Gala, a formal night benefiting a local domestic violence

Master of Ceremonies of the 2012 WRNG and longtime supporter of LLN – Jamarhl Crawford

Congresswoman Ayanna Pressley with local Boston 25 News – Investigative Reporter, Bob Ward at the 2012 WRNG

Antonio and myself with the 2012 WRNG Presenters and former
MA White Ribbon Day Coordinator – Craig Norberg-Bohm

agency. The event featured four men sharing how they use their voices to stand up and speak out against domestic violence, encouraging the other men in the room to do the same. At the end of the night's program, every man in attendance was asked to come to the front and recite the Massachusetts White Ribbon Day Pledge: "From this day forward, I promise to be part

CarLove share a moment at the end of the Inaugural WRNG - 2012

of the solution in ending violence against women and all gender-based violence." So many women in attendance that night, some survivors and others never affected by the issue, made a point to tell me how much it meant to see men take that stance.

The good times kept rolling as we received news early in March 2012 that LLN had received 501c3 non-profit status from the IRS. A few people had told me it was too difficult to complete the application on my own, so that determination letter was proof that I had proven those folks wrong.

Above: 2019 Heel-A-Thon – Heelers accompanied by local police

Attendee and LLN Supporter Rob Demeo proudly sports a pair of Mary-Janes he 'heeled' in, alongside survivor, Amy, and her daughter at the 2019 Heel-A-Thon

A Local Sorority participant 'Heeler'

Each quarter thereafter, we continued to up the ante with all the initiatives I had started during the year of pageantry. The Walk-A-Thon became the Heel-A-Thon, where men and women walk a mile on a busy street in (optional) high heels to help educate passers-by about the issue of abuse.

The Bedding Drive expanded beyond locally receiving new twin sheet sets and pillows. People and organizations from different states joined in, and the event now averages over 250 pieces of linen going back to local DV agencies every year.

Making speeches to community groups turned into Healthy Relationship Workshops that highlight relationship red flags, what constitutes a healthy relationship, how to safely exit a toxic relationship, and tips about how to

Bedding Drive Donations

become an active bystander against abuse. Love Life Now has presented to students at Harvard University as well as other college campuses, high schools, girls conferences, and corporation groups in person. Virtually, we have reached audiences as far as Saudi Arabia, parts of the Caribbean, and many groups across the United States.

While I have gone on to share my story with many outlets including CBS This Morning and *Huffington Post* Magazine, the core of my activism remains talking to people in my community about ways they can be part of eradicating domestic violence.

I never take for granted the voice that I found along the way, which now helps to empower others to find and use their voices to work toward a world free from abuse. To say that it is a privilege to do this passion work after God, is an understatement.

When I was set on this trajectory at the hands of my father, he never thought the end

*LLN's current Board Members –
Ebony, Antonio, Lovern and Rose
at one of the WRNG events*

result would be me dedicating my life to speaking out against all he did to us physically, verbally, and emotionally. It took a lot of work and introspection for this legacy to not be passed onto to my own family. Cutting ties with the trauma I experienced enabled me to connect the dots related to my family's history of violence. In doing so, I found my purpose and chose to Love Life Now, everyday, after God.

Very early on in the writing process for this book, suppressed memories and details forcefully resurfaced. I went through a range of overwhelming emotions that followed me to bed from my waking life. Many nights after I closed my eyes, I was plagued by brutal nightmares of me or my mother being attacked, or being surrounded by dead and dying murder victims. The anxiety from these dreams caused me to wake up in a cold sweat, afraid to fall asleep again for fear of encountering the violence. Even when I am fully awake and functioning I continue to be jumpy and easily startled. My subconscious thinks any sudden noise means someone is approaching to attack me, even though I am only surrounded by those who love and care about me.

The writing process placed me at a juncture where I had to fully accept that I could not deal with these emotions on my own, so I sought therapy. After finding a therapist that I felt like I could connect with, someone who addressed a lot of the things I had been experiencing, I am finally unpacking it all. Therapy has helped me realize that I may never be free from the trauma. My triggers present themselves in a variety of different ways, but now that I am taking care of my mental health, I can recognize and manage those triggers when they arise, which is invaluable.

I've also distanced myself from the idea that pleasing others gets admiration in return. I am more than enough. By not neglecting myself, I have been able to curate self-love and indulge in self care, both critical to the love I am able to pour out for others. I am forever grateful for that. If only Lloydie could see me now.

More than that, I wish he could see Mummy now. The one he sought so

Purple bouquet I flew in from Lee Lee's Creations as a tribute to Mummy's survivorship

Mummy in Trinidad on her 69th Birthday in 2020

hard to diminish with all of his power and control tactics. If only he could see that none of it won in the end, because she is still vibrant and full of life and continues to inspire others with her zest for life, sense of style, humor, and grace. She remarried in 2016, and I got to return the honor of walking her down the aisle on the day of her wedding. She beamed as a bride and our family loved sharing in her joy. She now resides in Trinidad and loves traveling. After all the chaos, her life is beautiful.

Post-traumatic stress disorder (PTSD) is a mental health condition that's triggered by a terrifying event — either experiencing it or witnessing it. Symptoms may include flashbacks, nightmares and severe anxiety, as well as uncontrollable thoughts about the event.

Most people who go through traumatic events may have temporary difficulty adjusting and coping, but with time and good self-care, they usually get better. If the symptoms get worse, last for months or even years, and interfere with your day-to-day functioning, you may have PTSD.

Source: *The Mayo Clinic*

ACKNOWLEDGMENTS

To my mother. My Mummy. Even on your darkest days, you carried us. You have shown me what it means not only to survive, but to THRIVE after God. I love you.

To my husband, Carson. You came into my life and brought an immense amount of unconditional love after God. Loving you is easy. Though it's not roses everyday, I thank you for helping me show our children what it means to be in a fully committed and caring relationship. Here's to a lifetime of laughter still ahead of us.

To our kids. I love you both so very much and whether you are near or far, know you're always in my heart. Continue to make the world a brighter place just by being YOU, after God.

To my girls. My bridesmaid crew, as well as Gaby, Tricia, my sister-cousin Jasmine, and notably my D. Thank you all for your genuine friendships that continues without fail. I cherish it more than you will ever know.

To every survivor I have met on this journey. We share a connection that binds us. Thank you for your bravery, strength, and resilience.

To my Love Life Now team and community. Thank you for always rocking with me and making the awareness possible.

ABOUT THE AUTHOR

Lovern resides in the state of Massachusetts with Carson and their two children. She continues to run the Love Life Now Foundation, focused on year-round awareness on the issue of domestic abuse.

CarLove and their 2 children

GET IN TOUCH WITH US:
Call / Text: 888.LLN.9876
www.lovelifenow.org
This Book on All Social Media: @TheLegacyHeLeftMe
Love Life Now on:
FB / IG: @lovelifenowfound
Twitter: @lovelifenowfoun
TikTok: @lovelifenowfound
The National Domestic Violence Hotline:
800.799.SAFE | www.thehotline.org